Dynamics of the Writing Conference

Dynamics of the Writing Conference

Social and Cognitive Interaction

Edited by

Thomas Flynn
Ohio University—Eastern

Mary King
University of Akron

National Council of Teachers of English
1111 W. Kenyon Road, Urbana, Illinois 61801-1096

Manuscript Editor: Jane M. Curran

Production Editor: Rona S. Smith

Cover Design: Doug Burnett

Interior Book Design: Tom Kovacs for TGK Graphics

NCTE Stock Number: 12811-3050

Library of Congress Cataloging-in-Publication Data

Dynamics of the Writing Conference; social and cognitive interaction / edited by Thomas Flynn, Mary King.
    p. cm.
    Includes bibliographical references and index.
    1. English language—Rhetoric—Study and Teaching. 2. Tutors and tutoring. I. Flynn, Thomas 1947-. II. King, Mary, 1941-.
PE1404.D9   1993
808'.024'07—dc20   93-12735
                                                    CIP

Contents

Preface   vii

I. Background and Theory

1. Promoting Higher-Order Thinking Skills in Writing
   Conferences   3
   Thomas Flynn

**II. Social Strategies: Building a Collaborative
   Relationship**

Introduction to Section II   17
   Mary King

2. A Counseling Approach to Writing Conferences   24
   David Taylor

3. Reevaluation of the Question as a Teaching Tool   34
   JoAnn B. Johnson

4. On the Issue of Authority   41
   David C. Fletcher

**III. Cognitive Strategies: Engaging Students in the
   Activities of Expert Writers**

Introduction to Section III   53
   Thomas Flynn

5. Looking for Clues   59
   Thomas C. Schmitzer

6. Experts with Life, Novices with Writing   62
   Marcia L. Hurlow

7. What Can Students Say about Poems? Reader Response in a
   Conference Setting   69
      Mary King

8. Using Conferences to Help Students Write Multiple-Source
   Papers   80
      Patrick J. Slattery

IV. Students Emerge as Independent Writers

Introduction to Section IV   91
   Mary King

9. Conferencing for the "Learning-Disabled": How We Might
   Really Help   95
      Cornelius Cosgrove

10. Fostering Spontaneous Dialect Shift in the Writing of
    African-American Students   103
       Susanna Horn

11. Writing Problems beyond the Classroom: The Confidence
    Problem   111
       Paula M. Oye

Index   121

Editors   125

Contributors   126

Preface

A hunter can see a buffalo, smell, taste, and touch a buffalo when the buffalo is completly inert, even dead, but if he hears a buffalo he had better watch out: something is going on. In this sense, all sound, and especially oral utterance, which comes from inside living organisms, is "dynamic."

—Walter J. Ong, *Orality and Literacy: The Technologizing of the Word*

The purpose of this collection of essays is to show how the social and cognitive interaction between students and teachers in writing conferences can promote the engagement of the higher-order thinking skills that students need to fulfill college writing requirements.

The idea for this book began rather simply: we decided to collect the best of the presentations made at East Central Writing Centers Association (ECWCA) conferences during its first ten years. Earlier versions of all ten essays in this collection have appeared previously in ECWCA conference proceedings, but we felt that a single volume would make these essays accessible to classroom teachers who face particular problems with students, such as those which inspired the investigations gathered here.

We determined to select those essays which address two fertile questions that underlie productive discussions of the conference approach to the teaching of writing: First, how do conferences between students and teachers actually work to foster growth in writing skills? Our review of the literature indicated that this topic has not yet received the attention that it deserves, and we feel that we have selected essays that do make a contribution to this field. And then a companion question arises: How can the teacher give control of the writing and of the conference itself to the writer in such a way that higher-order thinking is activated? These essays offer strategies that teachers can use to restrict their own exercise of power and to give students a greater share of responsibility in writing conferences.

"Promoting Higher-Order Thinking Skills in Writing Conferences," the general introduction to the book, provides background on research in individualized instruction, higher-order thinking, interaction between novices and experts, and characteristics of productive dialogue during writing conferences. The essays are grouped in three sections, which correspond to three primary features of instruction in higher-order thinking skills as they apply to the writing conference. The essays in section two, "Social Strategies: Building a Collaborative Relationship," focus on the powerful role that social interaction plays in human learning. In section three, "Cognitive Strategies: Engaging Students in the Activities of Expert Writers," the chapters demonstrate how teachers can use conferences to assist novice writers in mastering the expert habits of thought and practice that they will need in order to move from simply reporting or telling to transforming or creating knowledge. In section four, "Students Emerge as Independent Writers," the essays assert that direct instruction or attention to lower-order concerns may impede students and that higher-order thinking is the appropriate activity in writing conferences because it speeds writers' progress toward independent growth.

We wish to express heartfelt thanks to the East Central Writing Centers Association, which generously provided funds for copying and assembling the papers at the beginning of this endeavor, and to the members of its executive board, who made helpful comments and suggestions of the sort that are essential to writers.

In preparing a collection from a resource as rich as ten years of conference proceedings, one encounters many wonderful essays which deserve wider recognition; in the interests of preparing a concise, coherent text we have had to omit some excellent work. We must take full responsibility for such omissions, knowing the impossibility that we can fully appreciate every work or that one book can hold everything.

I Background and Theory

1 Promoting Higher-Order Thinking Skills in Writing Conferences

Thomas Flynn
Ohio University—Eastern

In this collection of essays we are contending that attention to the social and the cognitive aspects of writing conferences will enable teachers to use this pedagogy more critically, more productively. Writing center theorists such as Kenneth Bruffee, J. Trimbur, and Muriel Harris have made valuable contributions by focusing primarily on the social aspect of this pedagogy. But this perspective needs to be complemented by an awareness of the cognitive component of the tutorial as well.

For the last two decades, cognitive science has studied tutorials in order to build learning systems (Clancey 1982; Lepper and Chabay 1988; Ohlsson 1986; Sleeman 1982). The findings of researchers in this field have shed light on all applications of tutorials. It appears that the strength of the tutorial for promoting higher-order skills arises from three sources: the attention to cognitive skills, the social setting, and the instructional flexibility that it offers to the novice/student and the expert/tutor (Collins, Brown, and Newman 1989; Scardamalia and Bereiter 1985; Lajoie and Lesgold 1989). Appreciating the operation of these three elements in the writing conference will help us make it more effective and perhaps more commonly used. The essays collected here were selected because they show the sociocognitive aspects of the writing conference in operation. This introduction addresses the current perception of the writing conference and then, by examining an extended series of writing conferences, shows the role of cognitive and social factors in the success of that instruction. This approach contrasts with the usual practice within writing conference research of focusing on the social setting and dynamics. The work of theorists in this area (Bruffee 1986; Trimbur 1987; North 1987; Harris 1986; Reigstad and McAndrew 1984) has been fruitful and has elucidated some of the salient features of the writing conference:

- The student controls the direction of the learning.
- The focus of the session is on the student's writing skills, not on the text at hand.
- The short-term goal is to equip the student with the skills to surmount the difficulties that brought her or him to the writing center.
- The long-term goal is to enable the student to function independently when confronted with the writing tasks assigned in college (that is, to make the student a better writer).

These points describe an instructional process directed toward revealing and meeting the individual's needs. Intuitively, one might feel that conferencing ought to be an essential tool in writing instruction. But despite the recommendations of Garrison (1974), Graves (1983), and Murray (1968), the writing conference is not accepted as a central part of the curriculum for most teachers (Barker 1988).

Key among the factors that work against the acceptance of the writing conference are the limited research on this pedagogy, the more practical difficulty of spending adequate time with each student, and the lack of information on how best to use the time available. Despite the general restrictions on the amount of research on conferencing, some groundbreaking insights have been emanating from Sarah Warshauer Freedman and her associates (Freedman and Katz 1987; Freedman and Sperling 1985; Freedman 1987; Sperling 1990; Walker and Elias 1987).

These valuable efforts in the dynamics of the writing conference, however, have not been complemented by research on the comparative effectiveness of conferences and other modes of instruction. As a result, the few comparative studies of the writing conference have assumed disproportionate importance. Within composition studies, the strongest research-based argument against conferencing is a direct product of this neglect. In his meta-analysis of instructional modes, George Hillocks places conferences or tutorials under the category of "Individualized Mode of Instruction," which he broadly defines as that in which students "receive instruction through tutorials, programmed materials . . . , or a combination of the two" (1986, 126). As defined in this fashion, individualized instruction does not produce improvements significantly stronger than those achieved in the regular classroom.

Hillocks developed his conclusion using meta-analysis, a powerful research tool that permits the construction of wide-ranging findings by distilling common elements from many diverse research projects. At times, however, this procedure can yield unreliable results, as it has in this instance. The writing conference made a poor showing in Hillocks's analysis because few well-constructed investigations have been made on this pedagogy and because it was inappropriately categorized. The broad category of "Individualized Mode of Instruction" in which Hillocks placed the writing conference also contained much less effective modes of instruction, such as drill-and-review computer programs.

The second cause of the poor showing of conferences in Hillocks's analysis was that in 1986 Hillocks could find only one study that made full use of the resources of the writing conference (D. I. Smith 1974; cited in Hillocks 1986). In this study instructors worked with individual students to plan, organize, draft, analyze, rewrite, and evaluate papers. Although this process conforms more closely to the accepted notions of individualized instruction than the other studies that Hillocks surveyed, he felt compelled to drop this project from his analysis because it produced such strong improvement in student writing skills. If he had included it in the overall project, it would have distorted the survey's statistical validity (Hillocks 1986, 127). The practice in research of discounting extremes is designed to protect the core of the data from the influence of aberrant findings. In the interests of producing a comprehensive review of instructional methods, Hillocks was forced to turn to other, less conventional applications of the tutorial. Hillocks rightly notes serious flaws in these studies: in most of these projects the instructional process was not modified to take full advantage of the possibilities provided by interaction between a skilled teacher and a student. Instead, students were put through the regular curriculum one at a time. Their individual needs were not assessed, nor were instructional strategies constructed to meet their needs. Therefore, Hillocks's findings that individualized instruction is no more effective than regular classroom instruction are valid for situations where the only variable is the number of students undergoing instruction.

But it would be a serious oversight to assume that this evaluation applies to the work of expert tutors who possess a full array of instructional and interpersonal skills and who can shape them to the needs of an individual. Hillocks's dilemma—whether to publish conclusions on the basis of results from poorly designed studies or to ignore an important instructional method—forcefully shows the harm done by the neglect of the writing conference and emphasizes the need to determine the effectiveness of tutorials that take full advantage of the resources offered by one-to-one spontaneous interaction between a novice and an expert.

Fortunately, although further study needs to be carried out on the comparative benefits of the writing conference, the work on the theoretical aspects of the writing conference has been progressing well. Indirectly the writing conference has benefited from interest in the social construction of knowledge demonstrated by theorists such as Kenneth Bruffee and J. Trimbur. Assimilating information from diverse sources such as philosophers like Richard Rorty, anthropologists like Clifford Geertz, and educators like Paolo Freire, Bruffee, and Trimbur has made a strong case that the interaction between individuals can create knowledge and develop skills more effectively than reading or attending lectures. While this insight into the role of the social construction of knowledge could readily be applied to writing conferences between student and teacher, thus far the chief beneficiary has been the peer group, which makes obvious and dramatic use of social interaction. The writing conference, though offering similar social benefits and increased instructional advantages, has not yet experienced a similar enhancement.

Interdisciplinary Contributions to Understanding Conferences

The scant attention paid to the writing conference by composition theory and research has been offset by work within cognitive science and educational psychology. In these areas tutorials are beginning to be recognized as one of the most effective methods for instructing students in higher-order thinking skills, such as advanced literacy. Lauren Resnick's definition of higher-order thinking skills clarifies some aspects of writing instruction and indirectly makes the case for the value of tutorial instruction in this field. Resnick's key points are summarized below:

- Higher-order thinking often yields *multiple solutions,* each with costs and benefits, rather than unique solutions.
- Higher-order thinking often involves *uncertainty.* Not everything that bears on the task at hand is known.
- Higher-order thinking involves *self-regulation* of the thinking process. An individual cannot engage in higher-order thinking when someone else "calls the plays" at every step.
- Higher-order thinking involves *imposing meaning,* finding structure in apparent disorder.

- Higher-order thinking is *effortful.* There is considerable mental work involved in the kinds of elaborations and judgment required (1987, 3).

As this definition points out, writing, like other higher-order skills, is a strenuous, risky attempt by an individual to impose meaning on a situation that demands that he or she speak out. Invariably, I am reminded of Resnick's description of higher-order thinking when students speak with me about their writing: "I don't know what to do—I could use this material in my introduction, or I could save it for the conclusion" (*multiple solutions*); "I have all this research, but I haven't figured out what it adds up to" (*uncertainty*); "This is really difficult—I have written this section over three times, and I still am not satisfied with it" (*self-regulation*). Unfortunately, in many courses our students are not confronted with challenges as complex as these. Consequently, they lack the past experience, the role models, the schemas, the strategies, and the heuristics for solving these challenges. The writing conference between novice and expert provides strong benefits for this type of learning.

A review of the literature on higher-order thinking skills suggests that instruction in this area has three primary features:

1. It is *social* (Resnick 1987).
2. It provides for interaction between a *novice* and an *expert* (Spiro et al. 1988).
3. It trains students in the skills necessary to become *independent* learners (Bereiter and Scardamalia 1987).

The identification of writing as a higher-order thinking skill has important implications for instruction.

Analysis of a Writing Conference

The theoretical implications of developing advanced literacy skills through writing conferences that bring together a novice and an expert can best be understood through the analysis of actual practice. Paula Oye's account (in chapter 11 of this volume) of a successful tutorial incorporates the three elements mentioned above. This narrative covers Oye's experience during three academic quarters and thus provides an insight into the diverse improvements that extended writing conferences can achieve.

The *social component* was an essential ingredient in the success of this instruction. The writing center had been recommended to a student, referred to as Diane in this account, because her instructor felt that the strict structure and sharp demarcation of authority in the classroom did not suit Diane and that her classroom work could be supplemented by writing conferences. Simply appearing at the writing center, however, did not resolve Diane's difficulties. Oye first had to establish rapport with her student. Fortunately, she noticed that Diane was wearing a jacket from her own daughter's high school. This connection opened up a store of common associations and enabled Diane to feel more at ease. Oye was able to extend this trust, which had been established on a personal level, into professional matters and to encourage Diane to reveal more details about her subject and gradually work them into her written account.

The value of Oye's *expertise* is manifest in her ability to critique her performance and adapt her approach to her student's needs. Initially, when Diane had been reticent, Oye had responded by being directive. This tactic was effective in the short term because it enabled Diane to complete her assignment, but by concentrating on the task at hand rather than on the writer, it violated one of the rules of writing conferences. In the longer term, this intervention alienated the student and caused her to disown the paper and to give it only perfunctory attention. The tutor correctly analyzed her error and in subsequent conferences took care to foster Diane's efforts to take responsibility for her work. Oye also demonstrates technical expertise by flexibly adapting her demands to Diane's growing skill and confidence. *Flexibility* is at the heart of the successful writing conference.

In this narrative of a successful tutorial, the final element, *independence,* seems a natural culmination of the earlier efforts. Whereas at the beginning of her collaboration in the fall Diane had said, "I guess I just can't write," by the spring she was "aware of the process that she followed in writing a paper, and she could develop her ideas independently, confident of having something worthwhile to say." Oye scrupulously avoids taking all the credit for Diane's improvement, noting that Diane had the benefit of classroom writing instruction and peer group work for three academic quarters, but Oye feels that the confidence Diane gained in their writing conferences provided her with the impetus that she needed in order to find her own voice and speak for herself. Attendant with this process was an improvement in all other aspects of writing (grammar, structure, and vocabulary) even though some of those areas had not been discussed. (In chapter 10, Susanna Horn discusses the striking, spontaneous improvement in lower-order concerns that oftentimes accompanies improvement in higher-order skills.)

The Sociocognitive Foundations of the Writing Conference

The success achieved by this student and instructor is encouraging, but it sheds little light on the theoretical foundations of the writing conference. Why is *social interaction* an important component of learning in higher-order thinking skills like advanced literacy? What is there about the interaction between the *novice* and the *expert* that facilitates growth in these areas or domains? How is *independence* acquired or fostered in such skills? The answers to these questions may lie in recent work in cognitive science.

Social Component of the Writing Conference

The role played by social interaction has been debated in composition pedagogy. Linda Flower has attempted to bridge the gap between those who advocate the primacy of social factors in composition theory and those who believe the cognitive to be more significant (1989, 282). But her efforts have been hindered by the lack of information concerning how individuals learn in social situations. Lauren Resnick, however, has provided a firm beginning to this discussion by hypothesizing about the benefits that the social element offers learners, as summarized below:

1. The social setting provides occasions for *modeling* effective thinking strategies.
2. Thinking aloud in a social setting allows others to *critique* and shape one's performance.
3. The social setting provides *scaffolding* for a novice's initially limited performance.
4. The social setting *motivates* students.
5. The public setting also lends social status and *validation* to higher-order thinking (1987, 41).

Diane's impressive growth as a writer, visible through her conferences with Oye, testifies to the benefits of social interaction in writing instruction. The foundation of the interaction is dialogue, the immediate exchange of information. "Critical to the teaching-learning process is the role of dialogue; it is the means by which support is provided and adjusted" (Palincsar 1986, 75). In her dialogue and in her writing with her tutor, Diane could try out ideas and receive immediate response. Oye could also demonstrate appropriate ways to construct or assemble ideas and then withdraw this support as

Diane demonstrated her ability to function independently. As her continuing involvement in the writing center demonstrates, some aspects of the writing conference, perhaps the social as well as the academic or the cognitive, motivated Diane to pursue it voluntarily for a full academic year.

Novice-Expert Interaction in the Writing Conference

Another feature of the writing conference that distinguishes it from other modes of writing instruction is that it is built around dialogue. The close interaction that dialogue demands is the crux of this mode of instruction because it enables the student to announce his or her concerns and to shape the instruction to fit his or her needs. This talk also enables the teacher to provide limited, specific assistance, keyed to the writer's needs.

As David Taylor points out in chapter 2 of this volume, tutors can use conversation to put their students at ease, to establish a helping environment, and to facilitate learning. Care must be taken to use conversational strategies appropriately; when used inappropriately, such strategies can alienate the student and sabotage the conference. In chapter 3, JoAnn Johnson argues that the use of questions by instructors often has just this effect.

In addition to these interpersonal aspects, experts can use dialogue to serve a more directly pedagogical role, as Palincsar establishes in her analysis of the role of dialogue in matching tutor efforts to student needs (1986, 96). A productive dialogue has the following features:

1. It supports student contributions at the idea level, not the word level.
2. It uses student ideas deftly and links them with new knowledge.
3. It provides focus and direction to the dialogue.
4. It makes the point clear to the student.
5. It uses evaluative comments to transform student comments from negative to constructive.

The expertise necessary to engage in a productive dialogue does not come easily, but this volume offers a diverse collection of practices and insights which suggest how such expertise can be developed.

Fostering Independence through Writing Conferences

The ultimate goal of the writing conference is to develop competent, confident writers who resemble Diane after her year of conferencing. Like all writers, they will still benefit from discussing their work with other writers and readers, but as a result of their conferencing, they will be better able to direct the dialogue toward the features of the text that cause difficulty, and they will have developed a repertoire of strategies from which they can select the most appropriate. Though this self-assertive view of collaboration is essential to productive work outside of academia, to reach this stage of independence and authority students must struggle against the subservient, passive role assigned them in the traditional classroom.

Flanders (1970; cited in Palincsar 1986) reports that teachers are responsible for approximately 80 percent of all talk in the classroom and that at the secondary level they refer to student ideas only 3 to 9 percent of the time. In contrast, the writing conference strips away the paraphernalia of instruction and reduces it to its essence—the student, the teacher, and the student's manuscript. This reduction also removes from the teacher the crowd-control responsibilities that complicate the task of education when one tries to instruct twenty or more persons simultaneously.

Freed of the burden of complete responsibility for the class, the instructor can respond more authentically and more flexibly and can allow the student to assume control of the encounter. Sarah Warshauer Freedman and Anne Marie Katz have observed that conferences differ from purely social conversations in two aspects that signify that students are being encouraged to assert themselves. First, students interrupt tutors more often than most conversational partners do, which suggests that they are convinced of the importance of their contributions (1987, 72). Second, tutors observe longer silences than most participants in a conversation; these pauses provide students with additional time to reflect and plan their responses (78).

Of course, the goal of writing instruction, and all other higher-order skills, is for students to become independent, able to function on their own. The writing conference is peculiarly suited for this goal because it permits the flexible application of expertise, and it encourages growth in a structured environment. In a tutorial, an instructor can closely monitor student progress and provide scaffolding or support to assist the student in mastering new skills. Additionally, the instructor can readily withdraw that support to assure that the student does not become dependent on resources that will not be available when the student later must act alone.

The research and theorizing presented in this collection of essays assert the sociocognitive significance of the writing conference. Nonetheless, this pedagogy requires more studies that assess the flexibility, spontaneity, and richness inherent in encounters between novice writers and expert tutors.

Perhaps when that goal is met, classroom teachers will feel more comfortable and competent in moving the center of their instruction closer to the student.

Works Cited

Barker, E. Ellen. 1988. "The When, Where, How, and Why of Conferencing: A Summary and Interpretation of a Teacher Survey." ERIC Document Reproduction Service no. ED 297 327.

Bereiter, Carl, and Marlene Scardamalia. 1987. "An Attainable Version of High Literacy: Approaches to Teaching High-Order Skills in Reading and Writing." *Curriculum Inquiry* 17 (1): 9–30.

Bruffee, Kenneth A. 1986. "Social Construction, Language, and Knowledge: A Bibliographical Essay." *College English* 48:773–90.

Clancey, W. J. 1982. "Tutoring Rules for Guiding a Case Method Dialogue." In *Intelligent Tutoring Systems,* ed. D. Sleeman and John Seely Brown. New York: Academic.

Collins, Albert, John Seely Brown, and Susan E. Newman. 1989. "Cognitive Apprenticeship: Teaching the Craft of Reading, Writing, and Mathematics." In *Knowing, Learning, and Instruction: Essays in Honor of Robert Glaser,* ed. Lauren Resnick, 453–94. Hillsdale, N.J.: Lawrence Erlbaum.

Flanders, N. 1970. *Analyzing Teaching Behavior.* Reading, Mass.: Addison-Wesley.

Flower, Linda. 1989. "Cognition, Context, and Theory Building." *College Composition and Communication* 40:282–311.

Freedman, Sarah Warshauer, with Cynthia Greenleaf and Melanie Sperling. 1987. *Response to Student Writing.* NCTE Research Report no. 23. Urbana, Ill.: National Council of Teachers of English.

Freedman, Sarah Warshauer, and Anne Marie Katz. 1987. "Pedagogical Interaction during the Composing Process: The Writing Conference." In *Writing in Real Time: Modeling Production Processes,* ed. Ann Matsuhashi. Norwood, N.J.: Ablex.

Freedman, Sarah Warshauer, and Melanie Sperling. 1985. "Teacher-Student Interaction in the Writing Conference: Response and Teaching." In *The Acquisition of Written Language: Response and Revision,* ed. S. W. Freedman. Norwood, N.J.: Ablex.

Garrison, Roger H. 1974. "One-to-One: Tutorial Instruction in Freshman Composition." *New Directions for Community Colleges* 2:55–83.

Graves, Donald H. 1983. *Writing: Teachers and Children at Work.* Exeter, N.H.: Heinemann.

Harris, Muriel. 1986. *Teaching One-to-One: The Writing Conference*. Urbana, Ill.: National Council of Teachers of English.

Hillocks, George, Jr. 1986. *Research on Written Composition: New Directions for Teaching*. Urbana, Ill.: ERIC Clearinghouse on Reading and Communication Skills and National Council on Research in English.

Lajoie, Susanne P., and Alan Lesgold. 1989. "Apprenticeship Training in the Workplace: Computer-Coached Practice Environment as a New Form of Apprenticeship." Unpublished document. Pittsburgh: Learning Research and Development Center, University of Pittsburgh.

Lepper, M. R., and R. W. Chabay. 1988. "Socializing Intelligent Tutors: Bringing Empathy to the Computer Tutor." In *Learning Issues for Intelligent Tutoring Systems*, ed. H. Mandl and A. Lesgold. New York: Springer-Verlag.

Murray, Donald M. 1968. *A Writer Teaches Writing: A Practical Method of Teaching Composition*. Boston: Houghton Mifflin.

North, Stephen M. 1987. *The Making of Knowledge in Composition: Portrait of an Emerging Field*. Upper Montclair, N.J.: Boynton/Cook.

Ohlsson, S. 1986. "Some Principles of Intelligent Tutoring." *Instructional Science* 14:293–326.

Palincsar, Annemarie Sullivan. 1986. "The Role of Dialogue in Providing Scaffolded Instruction." *Educational Psychologist* 21:73–98.

Reigstad, Thomas J., and Donald A. McAndrew. 1984. *Training Tutors for Writing Conferences*. Urbana, Ill.: ERIC Clearinghouse on Reading and Communication Skills and National Council of Teachers of English.

Resnick, Lauren B. 1987. *Education and Learning to Think*. Washington, D.C.: National Academy Press.

Scardamalia, Marlene, and Carl Bereiter. 1985. "Development of Dialectical Processes in Composition." In *Literacy, Language, and Learning: The Nature and Consequences of Reading and Writing*, ed. David R. Olson, Nancy Torrance, and Angela Hildyard, 307–33. Cambridge: Cambridge University Press.

Sleeman, D. 1982. "Assessing Aspects of Competence in Basic Algebra." In *Intelligent Tutoring Systems*, ed. D. Sleeman and John Seely Brown. New York: Academic.

Smith, D. I. 1974. "Effects of Class Size and Individualized Instruction on the Writing of High School Juniors." *Dissertation Abstracts International* 35:2844A.

Sperling, Melanie. 1990. "I Want to Talk to Each of You: Collaboration and the Teacher-Student Writing Conference." *Research in the Teaching of English* 24 (3): 279–321.

Spiro, Rand J., et al. 1988. "Multiple Analogies for Complex Concepts: Antidotes for Analogy-Induced Misconception in Advanced Knowledge Acquisition." Washington, D.C.: Office of Educational Research and Improvement, Department of Education. ERIC Document Reproduction Service no. ED 301 873.

Trimbur, J. 1987. "Peer Tutoring: A Contradiction in Terms?" *Writing Center Journal* 11 (2): 20–30.

Walker, Carolyn P., and David Elias. 1987. "Writing Conference Talk: Factors Associated with High- and Low-Rated Writing Conferences." *Research in the Teaching of English* 21:266–85.

II Social Strategies: Building a Collaborative Relationship

Introduction to Section II

Mary King
University of Akron

Writing conferences which simply reproduce the interpersonal relationships of conventional schooling intensify teacher-centeredness, magnifying the teacher's authority and more powerfully denying the student any access to control. Our studies of the conference approach to the teaching of writing suggest a sharing of control between student and teacher. We are advancing a pedagogy for writing conferences based on the novice-expert relationship, since we are convinced by our own teaching experiences and those of the essayists reprinted here that this is how people best learn.

It must be recognized that in working with students in the kinds of writing conferences described in this book, teachers are asking students to perform in an unaccustomed role—the role of novice writer seeking advice from an expert. For teachers, too, this role of expert may be novel—it is more collaborative than the role of classroom teacher. The special value of this kind of writing conference is that—ideally—it replicates the way people learn most naturally: knowledge is constructed socially, in conversation; ideas are developed cooperatively. In a cooperative conversation, control is shared. The student controls the content of the conversation by proposing the topic to be discussed. The ideas being developed are those of the student, not the teacher. The teacher's part is to encourage pursuit of those ideas, to make analytic or defining statements about how the ideas are developing, and to provide information about the forms and purposes of academic discourse. The teacher gives expert guidance to the direction of the conversation.

In the first essay in this section, David Taylor shows how teachers can put aside their encumbering authority and assume a more helpful role. Then, JoAnn Johnson and David Fletcher analyze teachers' questioning behavior and demonstrate how teachers' accustomed patterns interfere with students' intentions. Together, these essays provide practical steps for establishing a helping relationship with student writers and show clearly why such steps are necessary.

Much of the theoretical basis for this departure from traditional teacher-student relationships is found in the work of Kenneth Bruffee (1984; 1986), Jerome Bruner (1986; 1990), Shirley Brice Heath (1983), and David Bleich (1988). Bruffee's contribution is to describe how knowledge is constructed through conversation; Bruner demonstrates that language is the building block for meaning making and also shows the integral connection between an individual's language use and the surrounding culture. Heath and Bleich point up the problem that formal schooling creates by disconnecting students from their home culture and from each other and by separating them from teachers: this practice frustrates learning. The social relations established in formal schooling are unfaithful to the true nature of human learning, which is founded in emotional and social ties to other members of the culture. We will return to these ideas.

It is appropriate at this point to consider three questions: What do we mean by the term *expert*? Expert at what? And how does the expert function differently from the way a teacher functions? To answer these questions, it is useful to identify what we mean by academic discourse, to look briefly at writing as a specialized use of language, and to think about some pedagogical implications of the social construction of knowledge, for these are the areas of expertise which concern us here.

A generic concept of expertise in writing can be depicted as a continuum with very general knowledge at one extreme (the novice's side) and specific kinds of knowledge at the other (the expert's side). According to Michael Carter, "Between the extremes of the global general knowledge of the rank novice and the fluent use of local knowledge by the expert, there is a range of knowledge that becomes increasingly local, of strategies that become increasingly domain-specific" (1990, 273). The expert, then, has a repertoire of strategies for high-level performance in a particular field or domain.

Domain-specific strategies of expert composition teachers are of two kinds: strategies for creating meaning through the act of writing and strategies for creating meaning socially by engaging students in conversations in which students create the knowledge they need.

A teacher working with a student in a writing conference must, of course, be expert at the practice of academic discourse, particularly academic writing. Broadly, we can say that academic discourse is reflective and analytical and has the goal of assigning meaning to the data under consideration. The expert is skilled in hearing, reading, and engaging in this specialized use of language, which is particularly characterized by a self-conscious reflectiveness. Martin McKoski identifies academic discourse as "speculative and exploratory in nature and cognizant of the complexity of any issue. It expresses stance and invites counterstance. It is the educated self" (1991, 9). We can also say that academic writing is distinct from speech in certain features, among them greater explicitness and elaboration, a hierarchal rather than merely sequential order of presentation, and an awareness of audience as "other," needing to have a context provided because it is unfamiliar with the circumstances of the writer's life and not privy to the writer's habits of thought (Olson 1977). Of course, postsecondary teachers have demonstrated expertise in written academic discourse in the normal process of obtaining credentials and thus admission to the academy.

A second area of expertise needed for conference teaching of writing is in the social construction of knowledge, the area opened up for composition studies by Kenneth Bruffee. Bruffee had taught college writing courses for years when the advent of open enrollment radically changed the academic setting, and he responded to the change as to a call for academic access and success. Researching the origins of knowledge, Bruffee synthesized the ideas of Thomas Kuhn, philosopher Richard Rorty, and anthropologist Clifford Geertz. Kuhn argues that scientific knowledge is created by the scientific community, while Rorty contends that all knowledge originates in social exchange; Geertz's studies in anthropology describe human cognition, perception, memory, and similar capacities as social in origin. Bruffee brought together viewpoints from these fields to illuminate what was for schools a radical idea: people, even students, talking together can create solutions to problems—can create new knowledge. Bruffee applied this principle, that students can learn from each other, to the teaching of writing in what has come to be called the Brooklyn Plan, now widely utilized throughout the United States in peer tutoring and classroom group work for all academic subjects and often renamed *collaborative learning.*

The research and theorizing which formed the basis for the Brooklyn Plan have continued to yield rich material on the function of language and culture in human learning. Jerome Bruner's *Actual Minds, Possible Worlds* (1986) and *Acts of Meaning* (1990) discuss the individual's developing use of language as a tool for constructing meaning. Bruner says that language is a tool shaped by the culture in which human beings participate by using that very tool, language. In fact, he says, it is participating in culture through language which actually creates us as human beings. He goes further yet, declaring that human culture has replaced the natural world as the shaping environment which controls the course of human development: "The divide in human evolution was crossed when culture became the major factor in giving form to the minds of those living under its sway. A product of history rather than of nature, culture now became the world to which we had to adapt and the tool kit for doing so." This view of the individual human being as a creature of culture, formed by verbal exchanges with other human beings, has radical implications, as Bruner points out. For psychology, this view "makes it impossible to construct a human psychology on the basis of the individual alone." For teaching, this view makes it impossible to ignore what Bruner calls "the realization of [human] mental powers through culture" (1990, 11–12), meaning that the richer the linguistic exchanges among individuals, the more completely their mental powers can be realized.

Language plays a powerful role, perhaps the most powerful of all aspects of the culture, in developing an individual's patterns of thought and verbal expression. Shirley Brice Heath demonstrates in *Ways with Words* (1983) how the verbal exchanges within two quite different American subcultures shape the mental habits and language use of group members differently and how these differences affect the children's behavior and success in school. If, then, we think of schools themselves as subcultures, we realize that great care must be taken about how the tool of language is used by those in authority and how its use is managed, rewarded, and forbidden to students. Verbal exchanges among students and teachers can promote exploration and growth—but they can also close students down emotionally and intellectually. David Bleich in the ethnographic passages of *The Double Perspective* shows this idea operating in the classroom; he discusses the connections between emotions and learning, and he argues that mutuality should replace individuality in a nonhierarchal classroom process. "Mutuality" here names "new social relations which can enable new access to authority for all classroom members" (1988, 253). The teacher in the classroom that Bleich describes retains the responsibility for shaping curriculum and deciding what the work of the class is to be—but this teacher functions as a participant in the classroom process, rather than as an authoritarian figure, so that everyone is a learner and all share in the construction of knowledge.

Teachers who wish to engage in writing conferences that promote thinking and learning at high levels need expertise in this area of sharing authority for the construction of knowledge with their students. But sharing authority is for many of us an unfamiliar teaching function. By the nature of our enterprise, we who teach are likely to concentrate our efforts on the information-processing function of language, and we often neglect the social aspect, which constructs and maintains relations among people. And yet the social function of language, because it distributes power, is of primary importance. And in a writing conference, the social relationship is intensified by the fact that the student is isolated with the teacher and deprived of the subculture of resistance provided by the presence of peers.

Constructing a useful relationship between student and teacher can ease the novice's entry into the conversation, which Kenneth Bruffee identifies as the main activity of academic life. Says Bruffee, "Reflective thinking is something we learn to do, and we learn to do it from and with other people" (1984). Assuming the authority required for this conversation is an unaccustomed burden for many college students, a burden that they naturally resist and one that teachers are often loath to share. It is helpful, then, to devote attention to the social as well as to the cognitive aspect of language.

The essays in this section explore some of the social consequences of language use between teacher and student in order to demonstrate that teachers can share control with their students by carefully and consciously crafting the part that each is to perform.

David Taylor's "A Counseling Approach to Writing Conferences" provides a model for the teacher, showing practical steps for creating a helping relationship to replace the more traditional teacher-student dialogue. Most of us are all too familiar with the futility of explicitly "teaching" students about language or writing, since students may or may not learn what we have taught. To expect them to do so is to engage in the *post hoc, ergo propter hoc* fallacy which Piaget called "magical thinking." Most of us have experienced this phenomenon both as teachers and as learners. Janet Emig, in her now-famous "Non-Magical Thinking: Presenting Writing Developmentally in Schools," declares that teachers of writing have "become the most magical thinkers of all," with their "relentless . . . efforts to teach writing" (1983, 22), when evidence suggests that "writing is developmentally a *natural* process" (25), which can be activated by an appropriate environment. Emig characterizes the school environment which can activate writing as "safe, structured, private, unobtrusive, and literate" (25). In his essay, Taylor shows how teachers, by using conferencing techniques adapted for our purposes from Carl Rogers, can develop such an environment and by doing so can engage student writers in a collaborative relationship characterized by commitment to language and ideas.

Building a collaborative relationship requires quite different techniques than those which teachers habitually employ—many of which may simply reproduce the relationship of the classroom. In "Reevaluation of the Question as a Teaching Tool," JoAnn Johnson reports on a study of writing conferences in a writing center. The study indicates that when the tutor asks questions, the tutor controls the conference, deprives the writer of responsibility, and may arouse emotions which divert energy from the work at hand. For all these reasons, questions should come from the student. Johnson suggests specific statements to make and directions to give which can result in longer, more reflective responses from student writers and which can help them deal with their writing problems.

At a less comfortable distance, David Fletcher, in "On the Issue of Authority," approaches the subject of questioning students by analyzing a student-tutor dialogue which demonstrates in painful closeup that their encounter is, in fact, a struggle for control. The student valiantly perseveres in thinking aloud, externalizing her analytic processes and demonstrating the kinds of opportunities that tutors have for helping students capitalize on their thinking—opportunities that, frustratingly, this tutor ignores. Each party to the exchange takes thirty-six turns, with the tutor devoting twenty-three of his turns to questions, mainly for the purpose of asserting his authority. As an antidote, Fletcher lists principles for teachers to follow in granting ownership of the ideas and the text to the writer during writing conferences.

Skillfully managed writing conferences present an opportunity to create optimal learning conditions, the kind of enabling environment which can activate student writing. The essays in this section show some techniques that teachers can use to promote thinking and writing—and some pitfalls to avoid.

Works Cited

Bleich, David. 1988. *The Double Perspective: Language, Literacy, and Social Relations.* New York: Oxford University Press.

Bruffee, Kenneth A. 1984. "Peer Tutoring and the Conversation of Mankind." In *Writing Centers: Theory and Administration,* ed. Gary A. Olson. Urbana, Ill.: National Council of Teachers of English.

_____. 1986. "Social Construction, Language, and the Authority of Knowledge: A Bibliographical Essay." *College English* 48 (December): 773–90.

Bruner, Jerome. 1986. *Actual Minds, Possible Worlds.* Cambridge, Mass.: Harvard University Press.

_____. 1990. *Acts of Meaning.* Cambridge, Mass.: Harvard University Press.

Carter, Michael. 1990. "The Idea of Expertise: An Exploration of Cognitive and Social Dimensions of Writing." *College Composition and Communication* 41 (October): 265–86.

Emig, Janet. 1983. "Non-Magical Thinking: Presenting Writing Developmentally in School." In *The Web of Meaning: Essays on Writing, Teaching, Learning, and Thinking,* ed. Dixie Gotswami and Maureen Butler. Upper Montclair, N.J.: Boynton/Cook.

Heath, Shirley Brice. 1983. *Ways with Words.* New York: Cambridge University Press.

McKoski, Martin. 1991. Unpublished draft of "Basic Writing Instruction: What Counts as Learning?" *Journal of College Reading and Learning* 23: 60–69.

Olson, David R. 1977. "From Utterance to Text: The Bias of Language in Speech and Writing." *Harvard Educational Review* 47 (August): 257–81.

2 A Counseling Approach to Writing Conferences

David Taylor
Moravian College

The strength of a writing conference—the opportunity for close interaction between a novice and an expert—can also bring about its failure. The goal of the conference is to provide inexperienced writers with the opportunity to discuss difficulties and to learn more effective strategies. But familiarity with the materials and extensive experience in solving writing problems can easily lead the expert to dominate the exchange and to provide the novice with new information but no new skills. In chapter 4 of this volume, David Fletcher offers an honest account of a conference that failed because the tutor's command of writing skills led him to ignore the student's real needs. In chapter 11, Paula Oye also describes an encounter in which a tutor inappropriately took control and misread a student's desires. Oye, fortunately, was able to rectify the situation and to reestablish the social contract.

The factor that jeopardized these conferences was not the tutor's lack of writing skills. Rather, it was the writing expert's lack of interpersonal skills, his or her inability to share the responsibility for the conference with the student and to adapt the pace of the instruction to the student's ability to absorb it. While writing conferences have been demonstrated to be an effective pedagogy for all students, both in the classroom and in writing centers, the students with whom we most often work on a one-to-one basis are those who are having difficulty, who are uncertain about their writing skills and about higher education in general. As Mike Rose describes such students in *Lives on the Boundary* (1989), they suffer from a wide range of personal, social, and academic anxieties. If we are to do full justice to the concept of knowledge as a social construction, we must develop skills in establishing an atmosphere of trust and in listening and understanding so that we com-

---

An earlier version of this essay appeared in the conference proceedings of the East Central Writing Centers Association for 1985.

prehend the significance of what the students say—not just for their text but for their sense of themselves as thinkers, as students. Like all teaching, conferencing is a perilous activity subject to many conflicting forces, and even though, as Lil Brannon (1982) reminds us, "we are not psychologists," I believe that teachers can surmount many of the problems that their authority causes by bringing to the conference a counselor's approach to structuring and conducting an interview with a client. The one-to-one conference is the primary workplace for psychological therapists and counselors. Much of their professional research and training is devoted to understanding what happens in conferences and to developing techniques for making conferences work. Some efforts have been made to tap this profession's know-how, but in light of the similarities between the counselor and the writing teacher, we need to develop this resource more fully (Thomas and Thomas 1989).

The aim of the therapist, according to Carl Rogers, is to release a client's capacity to deal constructively with life, thereby giving that person the power to resume control and to move forward. When reading that concept in Rogers's *Client-Centered Therapy* (1951), I was struck by the close parallel to the purpose of a writing conference on a student's early draft. The questions are essentially the same. The student may ask, "Where do I go from here?" or may admit, "I'm stuck and not sure what else to do. I don't feel that I'm being successful with this assignment." The teacher's job at that point is much the same as the counselor's—to put the student-client back in control so that she or he can move forward with a sense of clear direction. It is this power to take charge of writing—following through the stages of revision and editing—that our beginning writers lack.

A second similarity concerns the long-term goals of conferences. Counselor and client try to go beyond the immediate problem to develop the client's self-awareness and ability to react intelligently in new situations. The goal of therapy is to prepare for the future by dealing with the present. As teachers of the writing process, we also use the immediate problems of a specific assignment as a way to develop writing skills for the future demands of new writing situations. The counselor and the writing instructor, as the essays in section four of this volume point out, prepare the student to act independently in the future.

A third similarity involves the relationship between client and counselor, student and teacher. Because the aim of therapy is to help the client be in charge of his or her own life, the therapist assumes the role of growth facilitator rather than authority figure who dispenses solutions or directs behavior. In a counseling relationship, client and counselor are a collaborative team involved in what is often termed a "helping relationship." The counselor says, "Let's work together to attain an outcome that will help you be more in control of your life. Together we will try to understand what's bothering you, and together we will plan how to deal with it."

In a writing conference that has as its goal the enabling of the student to take charge of the writing process, there is this same collaborative relationship. Calvin Trillin once noted, "An editor should be someone who is trying to help the writer say what he wants to say" (1981, 15). It is much the same for a writing instructor in a conference. An important shift occurs from teacher as authority figure, who judges the product of writing, to someone who says, like the counselor, "I want to be involved with you in exploring what you're trying to say in this paper and in papers in the future. Together, I want us to find ways of writing effectively."

In short, sitting down with a student in a writing conference requires a different kind of teaching. As the other essays in this volume demonstrate, there are many facets to this type of teaching: social, cognitive, and disciplinary, among others; this essay addresses the social, which in many ways is the foundation for the others. In a conference we come together with the student in an intimate setting to help him or her deal constructively with sometimes intensely personal parts of life. This means that we have taken on, in important ways, the role of counselor in an interview. It is helpful, then, if we have at our disposal some of the insights, guidelines, and tools of the counselor. This information has for years been common knowledge for others in the helping professions—child care specialists, social workers, guidance counselors, psychologists, nurses—and should be common knowledge for teachers as well.

An introduction to this field includes the conditions necessary for a helping relationship, the characteristics of effective helpers, and the counseling skills for effective listening. A summary of these counseling concepts and skills that are appropriate in a writing conference appears in figure 1. The goal is to take what we are already doing naturally but perhaps unsystematically and, by becoming more conscious of what is involved in a helping relationship, to enhance our conferencing skills. Initially, these matters may not seem relevant to writing instruction, but as Oye points out in this collection's final essay, careful attention to these aspects of the conference can determine success or failure.

Conditions for the Helping Relationship

An often-stressed point in counseling literature is that the creation of *an atmosphere of acceptance and trust* is more important than a counselor's specific techniques. If the client believes that he or she can express feelings and attitudes freely, without threat of condemnation, then method is secondary. To create this climate, counselors use their primary helping tool—their own personality. There are three personality traits that are frequently identified as characteristic of effective helpers, traits that are almost entirely responsible for establishing acceptance and trust in a conference.

Helper Empathy. Like a counselor, a teacher needs a clear understanding of the reality of what the student is thinking. When students see that a teacher is taking the time to probe and to understand their meaning, they often gain a stronger sense of commitment to writing.

Helper Warmth and Caring. In a study that asked clients to identify the traits of an effective helper, there was strong agreement that the best helper is someone who responds enthusiastically to clients in a personal and concerned way (Brammer 1973, 29–35). A central value for these expert helpers was their stronger concern for people than for things (Combs et al. 1969). And, indeed, the teaching of writing as process means concentrating more on writers and their writing behavior than on the product they eventually produce.

Helper Regard and Respect. Rogers's description of this trait is "unconditional positive regard," by which he means that the client never feels threatened by a therapist's personal judgment (Rogers 1961, 283–84). There is no message that "I approve [or disapprove] of you or your writing." There is only the sense of acceptance of the individual and a willingness to help. In the first contacts especially, it is important to offer this regard and respect, saying in effect: "I want you to express yourself freely and to become the best writer that you can be on your own terms and not just to please me."

When an atmosphere of trust has been created, the teacher can make the shift from authority figure to collaborator; the benefits of this transition are impressive. There can be genuine, two-way talk about writing, perhaps for the first time in a student's life. If the student is assured of not being demeaned or judged in a personal way, the student can commit to writing without fear of being wrong, and the sluice gates of language and ideas open more. Through the process of establishing trust, the student-writer no longer remains a passive receptacle who is simply told to perform a prescribed intellectual function or to reproduce the thinking of the teacher. Instead, this

Summary of Counseling Concepts and Skills for Writing Conferences

Conditions for the Helping Relationship

    1. Atmosphere of acceptance and trust
- Helper empathy
- Helper warmth and caring
- Helper regard and respect

    2. Openness about the goals and process of the relationship

Stages in the Writing Conference

    1. Preparation and Entry
       Goals
- to open the conference with a minimum of resistance
- to lay the groundwork of trust

       Techniques
- use amenities to let student feel valued
- listen to chitchat for hints of academic or personal problems that may interfere with writing

    2. Clarification
       Goals
- to define the goals of the conference(s)
- to elicit student's reaction to the writing

       Techniques
- suspend diagnosis and encourage student's elaboration
- ask "what" instead of "why" questions

    3. Structuring
       Goals
- to make explicit the roles and responsibilities of the student and teacher
- to indicate the steps to be followed in reaching the goal of the conference

    4. Exploration
       Goals
- to read the draft holistically
- to encourage the student to explore his or her own thoughts and writing
- to help the student identify specific writing problems

       Techniques
- read the draft aloud, without stopping for comments or written notations

- use general and specific questions that lead the student to an expanded self-awareness of the writing

5. Consolidation
   Goals
   - to state specifically what needs to be done to the writing
   - to provide explanation and teach skills for revising

6. Planning and Termination
   Goals
   - to summarize the accomplishments of the conference(s)
   - to set deadlines and anticipate the next conference
   Techniques
   - ask the student to bring together for himself or herself the outcomes of the conference
   - talk about the next conference in order to give a sense of moving forward positively and working toward a future goal

Skills for Listening and Understanding ("Listening with the third ear")

1. Paraphrasing
   Goals
   - to restate the student's message in similar but fewer words
   - to test one's understanding of what was said
   - to show the student he or she has been understood
   Techniques
   - listen for the basic message of the student
   - restate to the student a concise and simple summary of the basic message
   - observe a cue or ask for a response from the student that confirms or disconfirms the accuracy and helpfulness of the paraphrase

2. Perception Checking
   Goals
   - to guess a basic message and ask for verification of it
   - to bring vague thoughts into sharper focus
   - to correct misconceptions of the student's message
   Techniques
   - admit confusion about the student's meaning
   - paraphrase what you think you heard
   - ask for confirmation directly from the student
   - allow the student to correct your perception if it is inaccurate

Figure 1. Summary of counseling concepts and skills for writing conferences.

is someone who is ready to use writing to discover what she or he genuinely thinks and feels about the world. The student is ready to "write for surprise," as Donald Murray puts it (1984).

Skills for Listening and Understanding

Counselors must develop several clusters of skills—those for providing comfort, intervening in a crisis, modifying behavior, and leading clients to solve personal problems and make important decisions for themselves. Most useful to writing teachers are the set of skills for understanding the client and for helping that person understand himself or herself. Four of these skills for listening and understanding are discussed below: paraphrasing, perception checking, leading, and summarizing.

It seems odd to talk about what comes naturally—just listening to and understanding what someone says. But a heightened kind of listening is required in a counseling interview or writing conference. This intensive listening is not a passive process but an active one, calling for sharply focused attention and sensitivity to the words and behavior of another. Developing this sensitivity is a matter of listening to meanings beneath the words, tone, and gestures of a speaker, or in psychologist Theodor Reik's well-known phrase, "listening with the third ear" (1948). By this he means focusing attention beyond what someone is saying or doing in order to comprehend the meanings or perceptions that are producing that behavior.

A technique for developing the third ear is to ask oneself questions while listening: "What is this person's message to me?" "What is he trying to say to me with those words and that tone?" "What does she want me to know about her?" So strong is the tendency to impose our own structure or meaning on what someone says that this conscious effort is required to be open to the reality of what someone is saying.

Such concentration upon the person's real meaning is characteristic of effective helpers, for it provides what Carl Rogers calls "the recognition and acceptance of feeling." With this kind of listening we cultivate a sensitivity that allows a truer understanding and acceptance of others. Most importantly, the very experience of being listened to in this way is strongly therapeutic in itself. We have the power to further growth in others, whether it be growth in writing or emotional growth, simply by being a sympathetic listener who does nothing else but help others understand themselves (Combs, Avila, and Purkey 1977).

Paraphrasing, the first listening skill, is an attempt to restate the client's basic message in similar but fewer words, as shown in the following example:

Client: I just don't understand. One minute she tells me to do this, and the next minute to do that.

Counselor: She really confuses you.

Client: Yeah, she sure does, besides . . .

Paraphrasing allows the teacher to test an understanding of what was said, show the student this understanding, and help the student to clarify what she or he thinks and feels:

Student: I'm gonna flunk English 100. The teacher gives me an F on a paper and tells me to write it again. I write it again and get another F.

Teacher: You really seem frustrated. You turn in a paper and you are told to write it again.

Student: I don't mind writing it again. It's not knowing what he wants.

The example illustrates full listening to a person's message, followed by a reflection of that message. Feeling understood in turn encourages the student to probe deeper, to elaborate. Paraphrasing is thus a potent instrument for opening the channels of self-insight.

Perception checking is different from paraphrasing in that the teacher first admits confusion; then the teacher guesses the student's basic message and asks for an affirmation of that guess. In this way, perception checking helps the student to bring vague thoughts into sharper focus and clears the way for an accurate understanding of the student's thoughts. The following exchange brings together a paraphrase and a check of perception:

Teacher: You have a lot to say about hospitals. Let's try to bring it together. What would you say is the thesis of your essay?

Student: About how most people are afraid of hospitals because they're afraid of what doctors might do to hurt them.

Teacher: So, the thesis is "fear of hospitals is caused by fear of pain."

Student: That's the big part. But also there's just not knowing what will happen to them.

Teacher: Let me try to understand. Now you say there is a second reason for the fear of hospitals—anxiety or fear of the unknown. Is that part of it, too?

Student: Sure, you're in danger, at least so far as your health, and you're afraid of not getting well. It's hard when you don't know, waiting there.

The exchange indicates the value of suspending evaluation while merely trying to understand fully and precisely what the student wishes to say. In this way, the teacher facilitates the student's own discovery and clarification of thought in his or her own words.

To *lead* is to invite verbal expression along desired lines. The goal of *indirect leading* is to get the student started and to keep the responsibility on him or her for keeping the conference going. An example would be the statement "Perhaps we could start by your telling me how this assignment went for you," which gives the student the responsibility for identifying what needs to be dealt with first. Later on, indirect leading would take the form of "Tell me more about that," followed by an expectant look. A *direct lead,* on the other hand, asks the student for precise information: "Are there other causes for the fear of hospitals?" or "Give me a specific example of that." Both indirect and direct leading encourage the student to elaborate, clarify, or illustrate what was said. And because of the open-ended questions and statements used, both forms of leading keep responsibility on the student for clarifying and developing his or her own thoughts.

The purpose of *summarizing* is to give the student a sense of moving carefully through a conference step by step and to consolidate the progress made. A student usually can and should do some of the summarizing. A teacher might ask: "How does our work look to you at this point? Try to pull it together briefly" or "Sum up for me what you'll be doing with this paper in the next draft." Summarizing thus tests a student's understanding and also keeps responsibility for the writing on the student. At times the teacher may wish to do the review, especially midway during a conference: "So far we've talked about developing your thesis with more examples. Now let's give some attention to the order of those paragraphs." Finally, a summary of a previous conference can be used at the beginning of a new one to provide continuity: "In our last conference we talked about making the paragraphs fuller and more focused. Let's see how they came out."

An additional advantage to creating a mood of understanding is that it narrows the gap between powerless student and powerful teacher. Now the student must seriously consider a teacher's questions about the piece of writing and must assume responsibility for answering them. Since the teacher will not be giving commands or dispensing solutions, the only alternative for the student is to think, write, and inquire until he or she discovers a solution.

Works Cited

Brammer, Lawrence. 1973. *The Helping Relationship: Process and Skills.* Englewood Cliffs, N.J.: Prentice-Hall.

Brannon, Lil. 1982. "On Becoming a More Effective Tutor." In *Tutoring Writing: A Sourcebook for Writing Labs,* ed. Muriel Harris. Glenview, Ill.: Scott, Foresman.

Combs, A. W., D. L. Avila, and W. W. Purkey. 1977. *Helping Relationships: Basic Concepts for the Helping Professions.* 2d ed. Boston: Allyn and Bacon.

Combs, A. W., et al. 1969. *Florida Studies in the Helping Professions.* University of Florida Social Science Monograph no. 37. Gainesville: University of Florida Press.

Murray, Donald. 1984. "Writing and Teaching for Surprise." *College English* 46: 1–7.

Reik, Theodor. 1948. *Listening with the Third Ear: The Inner Experience of a Psychoanalyst.* New York: Grove Press.

Rogers, Carl. 1951. *Client-Centered Therapy: Its Current Practice, Implications and Theory.* Boston: Houghton Mifflin.

_____. 1961. *On Becoming a Person.* Boston: Houghton Mifflin.

Rose, Mike. 1989. *Lives on the Boundary.* New York: Penguin Books.

Thomas, Dene, and Gordon Thomas. 1989. "The Use of Rogerian Reflection in Small-Group Writing Conferences." In *Writing and Response: Theory, Practice, and Response,* ed. Chris M. Anson, 114–26. Urbana, Ill.: National Council of Teachers of English.

Trillin, Alice. 1981. "A Writer's Process: A Conversation with Calvin Trillin." *Basic Writing* 3:5–18.

3 Reevaluation of the Question as a Teaching Tool

JoAnn B. Johnson
University of Akron

Asking questions to spark discussion from students is a time-honored practice of teachers. But as David Fletcher makes clear in chapter 4, there is empirical evidence to show that asking questions to engage the student's thinking during a writing conference may have the opposite effect. On a social level, questioning can jeopardize the mood of empathy, trust, and respect that David Taylor argues in chapter 2 we should be trying to establish. The literature on question asking reveals three problems associated with this practice: First, the person asking the questions controls the direction of the inquiry; therefore, the student should be asking the questions. Second, questions imposed by a teacher may derail the student's train of thought, introducing confusion. Finally, most teachers do not give students as much time as they need to respond fully to questions. Teachers who become sensitive to these problems may want to ask fewer questions and find other means of communicating with students about their writing. Making declarative statements, especially paraphrases, and using imperative sentences often invites longer, more reflective responses.

Observing students working on various writing tasks in a university writing center sheds some light on this phenomenon. When a student arrives at a writing conference, he or she may bring a mass of confusing information plus a lack of, or loss of, strategies for problem solving. When the student presents this information to the tutor, the focus of attention looks somewhat like model 1 in figure 2, with both tutor and student focused on the problem. After a few moments of questioning by the tutor, the focus of attention changes to that shown in model 2 of figure 2 because the tutor has become engaged with the problem by becoming aware of the point of error. The tutor then

An earlier version of this essay appeared in the conference proceedings of the East Central Writing Centers Association for 1984.

34

begins to untangle the problem while the student's attention is focused on the tutor and his or her problem-solving strategy. But if the student is to develop his or her own strategies, the structure of the conference should take the shape of model 3 in figure 2, with the student addressing the problem and the tutor listening to the student.

These three models of a tutoring conference deserve our attention because they show the position of a necessary component in the process of a learning experience. This element is often referred to as a questioning attitude. Jean Piaget used the more clinical term *dissonance*, an imbalance that needs to be set right. In model 1 of figure 2, the presence of dissonance is greater in the tutor than the student. At this point the tutor genuinely feels a need to know. The student, on the other hand, has given up on his or her own questioning strategies. In model 2, the tutor has found the source of the dissonance and is engaged with his or her own need to correct the imbalance by using his or her own problem-solving strategies. Unfortunately, the student is also engaged in the tutor's strategies. In model 3, which portrays the goal of the writing conference, the student is engaged with the source of dissonance, thus developing his or her own problem-solving strategies, and the tutor is observing the student.

Psychologists such as L. S. Vygotsky, Jean Piaget, Carl Rogers, and Jerome Bruner have brought into sharper focus a key concept of cognition that is of major importance to our understanding of the relationship between the question and learning. By various paths, each of the above psychologists has linked the concept of learning involvement with an awareness of dissonance. Learning arises out of a puzzlement or question within the individual. It is an accepted principle that the degree of learning is directly related to the degree of the learner's involvement; however, we find that creating that in-

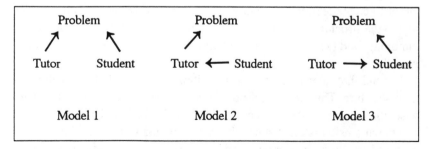

Figure 2. Three models of a tutoring conference.

volvement in another person is difficult, if not impossible. Since we are aware that for learning to take place, questions must arise within the learner, we as tutors try to create a questioning attitude by adopting the traditional Socratic method and asking questions. This we should not do.

In the University of Akron Writing Center, it was long our practice to use the question not only as a measuring device to determine the student's level of knowledge but as a means of encouraging the student to verbalize or elaborate on the strengths and weaknesses of his or her work. To evaluate the success of our practice, we planned a small study.

An analysis of randomly taped sessions at the Writing Center proved enlightening; certain patterns began to appear. For instance, a short-answer pattern was established in a first meeting when, in an attempt to create some measure of rapport, a tutor asked get-acquainted questions about the student's hometown, course of study, future goals, and the like. And though these questions were intermingled with relaxed personal reflections from the tutor, the student gave only short, specific answers. The tapes also revealed that the type of questions most used in relation to the student's work were those requesting short answers. Out of this sample of 232 questions, 64 percent were requests for factual information and 23 percent were requests for paraphrasing, rereading. Many of these questions were answered in haste by the tutor, who did not wait for the student's response. If the information was known by the student, the answer came quickly but was limited. At other times no answer was given, and the resulting tension remained high until the silence was broken. Significantly, it was the tutor who most often broke the silence, and very often with another question.

Disappointed with the large percentage of fact-requesting questions, I made the question the next target of study. I found that if we accept the theory that learning begins at the point of dissonance or felt need within the learner, then the often-used technique of questioning the learner in an attempt to create learning is not a valid tool for two reasons: (1) the power within the structure of a question and the restrictions of its response can be inhibiting, and (2) the necessary *felt need* for learning involvement is misplaced.

I found that questions have an inhibiting power through the nature of their structure. They require, if not demand, a response for closure; otherwise, the tension created by the question remains high and unresolved. An additional tension is created simply by responding to the question, for responses have limitations or boundaries. In this case the boundaries are determined by the questioner, who thus deprives the student of control. Questions requiring factual answers limit responses to facts known only by the questioner, the responder, or possibly by both. An analysis or evaluation response is limited through the available information from which to work, and until the responder receives some signal from the questioner that he or she has given a satisfactory response, the danger of error remains high. Consequently, the inhibiting power of the question and the boundary limitations of the response restrict thinking rather than release it. J. T. Dillon cites eleven studies that show question responses are typically brief, a single word or phrase, and that as further questions are posed, responses tend to become shorter (1978, 56).

Some types of questions, it seems, have a more inhibiting nature than others because decoding carries an emotional as well as informational message. For instance, the "Why" question often receives a hesitant answer or the response "I don't know," possibly because it seems to imply error before an analysis has begun. In *The Helping Interview* (1981), Alfred Benjamin gives an interesting theory for this phenomenon. It appears that "Why" is generally the first question asked of a child when he or she *has* done something wrong, reminding us of the theory that memory apparently travels along affective paths, with the "feeling generating memory and memory generating feeling." We are all too familiar with the overriding power of the emotional message as opposed to the informational message of a teacher's marginal notes or questions on a returned paper, which students assume are harshly critical even without reading them. Furthermore, understanding what the question means is sometimes difficult for the student. After all, there are innumerable decoding possibilities based on what the student brings to the conference, and the inhibiting power of a question can be intensified by the student's reasoning at that moment. A student may decode the question with another question composed around a concern for the reason for the tutor's question. A chained sequence of decodings, such as, "Why is he asking *that* question?" or "Why is he asking *me* that question?" is an intrusion into any problem-solving strategies that the student may have had, and the tutor's question now has become "Threatening, paralyzing, [embarrassing] or even may be considered an attack" (Dillon 1982, 138). Janet Moursund points out that the student who hears the question "is not a passive machine, carrying on a running translation of sound. Listening is an active process in which every message fragment is screened and either accepted or rejected (and possibly highlighted) so as to fit whatever else is going on in the listener's thoughts and feelings" (1976, 83). The tutor has no way of knowing at what emotional level the student is attending the question.

The Writing Center tapes also revealed a separate yet related area of inhibition—the amount of wait-time permitted by the questioner between question and response. In 1974, Mary Budd Rowe published the results of a six-year investigation into the influence of teacher/pupil wait-time ranging from 0.9 seconds to 3–5 seconds. Her analysis of recorded classroom sessions revealed that student response changed in ten variables, eight of which apply directly to the conference session. Rowe found that with increased wait-time, (1) the length of response increased; (2) unsolicited but appropriate responses increased; (3) the failure to respond decreased; (4) confidence, as reflected in response, increased; (5) speculative responses increased; (6) evidence inferences increased; (7) student questions increased; and (8) responses from students rated as slow increased. She also found that as wait-time increased, the length of student response increased *concurrently* with inferences connected to evidence. Rowe concluded: "It is as though the mapping of experience and thought into language proceeds in pieces. Intrusion between the bursts by another [person] prevents the expression of a complete sequence" (1974, 87). Clearly, then, giving students enough time to respond is an important part of teaching, and we should stretch that time as much as we can in order to give our students opportunity to think.

There are many ways of cutting off wait-time, but I believe that the question, by its very nature, is extremely intrusive. It places an extra decoding burden on the student, resulting in various degrees of cognitive strain. When the student is slow to respond, often the tutor interrupts the student's cognitive activity with further questioning in an attempt to clarify, intensifying the cognitive strain by layering decoding on top of encoding processes. If the concepts within the original question are new to the student, his or her decoding processes are somewhat slower, and the encoding into a syntactically acceptable response will need more time. Intrusive questions simply add extra message sets to be decoded before the student has completed the first. It seems reasonable to assume, then, that unsolicited interference in the student's cognitive activity is counterproductive to the intended goal of student cognitive involvement, and that longer wait-time has positive measurable influence on student response; therefore, we should not interrupt our students' thinking with further questions.

The second major reason that the question is not a valid tool for creating dissonance in the learner is needs location. When the tutor composes a question for the student, it is based on the tutor's perception of need within the student; consequently, the attention of both student and tutor are focused on what the tutor chooses as need. If, on the other hand, the student composes the question, it is based on what he or she chooses as need. For instance, if the tutor asks, "Why did you put a comma here?" it draws attention to an error, or it requests an answer that is rule bound. If, however, the student asks, "Do I need a comma here?" he or she has chosen the point of discussion that is at that moment his or her felt need.

Some of the literature dealing with the question as a teaching tool concentrates on the cognitive level of expected response, claiming that questions structured a given way will elicit responses on a desired level; however, Dillon (1982) sheds doubt on the question as a catalyst for predetermined cognitive activity in anyone other than the questioner. Students often respond on a different level than expected, giving a short answer when a long evaluation is desired, so there is no guarantee that a question will cause a predetermined level of response.

Dillon points out that education is the only profession that considers the question a stimulant for higher levels of thinking (129). Professionals such as pollsters or trial attorneys use the question to control or inhibit thinking. In contrast, such professionals as counselors or psychotherapists, who have a purpose similar to that of educators—free expression of thought—purposefully avoid the question because it inhibits thought and responses.

Since there are so many negative qualities to the question, it would seem logical to avoid asking questions as much as possible in a tutoring session. But how? Dillon and others found that making statements created longer, more reflective responses. Paraphrasing by the tutor is excellent because it forces the student to consider deep structures, highlighting the success or failure of various sections of a written piece. However, the imperative sentence structure is the most productive strategy for a writing conference. If a student is told to *explain* the assignment made by the teacher, *read* a section aloud, *point* to the places that are creating discomfort, or *experiment* by writing an idea in different structural styles, then the student will be dealing with his or her needs by elaborating, manipulating, and developing strategies for the identification and solving of his or her writing problems, which is the goal of a writing conference.

In the next essay in this collection, David Fletcher analyzes a conference in which tutor questions played a major role and in which, consequently, the student's goals were not discerned, and her problems, left unidentified, were not solved. Asking questions has traditionally been a major component of teaching strategies; however, if the student is to become involved with the learning experience in a productive manner, the questions must come from the student.

Works Cited

Benjamin, Alfred. 1981. *The Helping Interview.* 3d ed. Boston: Houghton Mifflin.

Dillon, J. T. 1978. "Using Questions to Depress Student Thought." *School Review* 87 (1): 50–63.

_____. 1982. "The Effect of Questions in Education and Other Enterprises." *Journal of Curriculum Studies* 14 (2): 127–52.

Moursund, Janet P. 1976. *Learning and the Learner.* Monterey, Calif.: Brooks/ Cole Publishing Company.

Rowe, Mary Budd. 1974. "Wait-Time and Rewards as Instructional Variables, Their Influence on Language, Logic and Fate Control: Part One—Wait-Time." *Journal of Research in Science Teaching* 11 (2): 81–94.

4 On the Issue of Authority

David C. Fletcher
New York University

What is there in the relationship between the tutor and the student in the writing conference that moves the student toward intellectual growth and intellectual autonomy? Within this larger question, we must consider a few related questions: How is authority manifested? To what extent are authority and ownership granted to the student? What is the role of the teacher or tutor in accomplishing the empowerment of the student?

The working premise for the model of transaction between the tutor and student in which authority is negotiated and shared is that the purpose of the writing instructor should be to take the intentions and the aims of the writer seriously and, in doing so, to acknowledge the writer's authority through writer-instructor dialogue.

This model of transaction means that student writers must follow an instructor's suggestions only when students decide that these comments assist them in developing their intentions and meanings. This tenet creates a difficult problem for those of us who have been trained to exert authority by assuming ownership of the student's text. However, such an exercise of authority interferes with the intellectual development of our students and should therefore be avoided.

In this essay, I analyze the opening dialogue of a single tutorial session. This analysis is designed to enable writing tutors to determine the extent to which they are, in fact, granting the writer authority and, conversely, the extent to which they are taking away that authority and initiative by telling the writer what to say and when and how to do so. This essay differs from the other essays in this collection in that they demonstrate the value of tuto-

An earlier version of this essay appeared in the conference proceedings of the East Central Writing Centers Association for 1985.

rials by presenting positive examples of tutors who realize that though they possess greater technical skills than their students, those assets are valuable only if employed by the students to express what they themselves want to say. In contrast, this essay shows the value of those approaches that emphasize the student's drive to create meaning by putting these expert social strategies in relief, by showing how a writing conference can founder when the tutor loses sight of those principles. Though written independently of JoAnn Johnson's essay on the negative effects of questions in a conference (chapter 3), the dialogue reported here seems almost to have been written to illustrate the harm that interrogation can wreak on a writing conference. In the thirty-six exchanges of dialogue, the tutor asks twenty-nine low-level or fact-based questions, while the student asks only four questions, all of which are direct responses to tutor questions and attempts to clarify his meaning. Johnson observes that the question places the questioner in control and requires that the questioner's needs be met. The tutor in the following conference declares his adherence to the principle of granting authority to the writer, but a close examination of his words and actions reveals the disparity between his ideals and his practice. The following questions guide my analysis of this writing conference:

1. Is attention given to the subjective meanings that the writer brings to the session, and is the writer assisted by the tutor in developing these meanings?
2. Does the tutor attend to the writer's purposes and choices?
3. Is attention given to the disparity or congruency between what the writer has written and what he or she intended?
4. Is the opportunity created within the conference for the writer to clarify or refine the relationships between effect and intention?
5. Are suggestions and strategies offered by the tutor to assist the student in developing his or her intentions?

To determine the answers to these questions, I attend to the differing subjects that the student (S) and the tutor (T) focus on during the session. By differentiating their focal points, I identify points of reference and cues that the student provides for the development of her text. These markers enable us to judge how well the tutor acknowledges and works with these cues and how well he uses his expertise and interpersonal skills to help the student with her writing assignment.

T.1:   Hi.

S.1:   Hi.

T.2:   Now, what can we do today?

S.2:   Well, the assignment . . .

T.3:   Already . . .

S.3:   On a piece of art . . .

T.4:   I didn't hear . . .

S.4:   On a piece of art . . .

T.5:   On a piece of art. What is the assignment?

S.5:   The name of the assignment?

T.6:   Uh hum.

S.6:   Well, basically, we have to respond to a piece of art and try to analyze our response.

T.7:   So it is to respond to a piece of art?

S.7:   Right, that is the first point . . .

T.8:   And then the second point?

S.8:   Um, write our response, like how is our response based on our family values, what caused you to respond to that piece of art in that manner? And we also have to do a bit of research, and in our response we have to know if the research helped our response, helped in the way . . .

T.9:   Which response, the first or the analysis?

S.9:   Um, if, no, if the research helped our response to a piece of art. Researching the artist . . .

T.10:   Do you do the research before you respond, after you respond in terms of how you yourself respond to? Where, at what point does the research come in?

S.10:   We were supposed to do research before we start writing our paper, but I didn't. I couldn't find anything until after I wrote the first draft. So the first draft is simply my interpretation of the piece, my response.

T.11:   I think that is the best way to start.

S.11:   My response . . .

T.12:   Then you can get that one down and then . . .

S.12:   I did research on Ben Shahn. And basically what I found was . . .

In lines S.3, S.6, and S.8, the student, by introducing her assignment, provides the first cue for the instructor to become involved in the text. But the tutor does not pursue the student's understanding of the meaning that she

has made of the assignment. Just as Johnson predicts, exploration of the
student's use of the assignment is curtailed by the tutor's pattern of questions beginning with T.5 and continuing through T.10. Each time the student
attempts to explain the assignment and formulate her interpretation (S.8 and
S.9), the tutor (T.10, T.11, and T.12) uses a comment or question to redirect
the writing conference. Interestingly, the tutor did not follow the advice that
he was giving the student about the need to develop her own interpretation.
He appears to be using his conversational turns to assert ownership of the
session.

The next portion of the conference shows a similar struggle for domi-
nance:

> *T.13:* Wait, wait, let's, let's, let me ask you a couple questions and then we
> can come back to what your research is.
>
> *S.13:* Okay.
>
> *T.14:* So what, what is the purpose of your text?
>
> *S.14:* You mean the assignment?
>
> *T.15:* Yes, the, what is the purpose of your paper?
>
> *S.15:* To, what should I say? To look at the piece and that is it.

Again, as in the previous exchange, the tutor initiates a series of questions,
which take the student away from her attempts to discuss the assignment in
S.11 and S.12, "I did research on Ben Shahn. And basically what I found
was . . ." Clearly, the tutor is establishing his own agenda with this series of
questions that take the student away from a discussion of her writing to a
discussion of the tutor's concerns. This exchange and the questions that follow lay out a pattern of rhetorical questions whose meanings for the student
are not actively investigated. At T.13, "Wait, wait, let's, let's, let me ask you
a couple questions and then we can come back to what your research is," we
see the tutor's preference for his questions rather than for the student's exploration and development of the assignment. In response to T.14, "So what,
what is the purpose of your text?" we see that the student (S.14 and S.15)
does not understand this question and again gives an explanation for the
assignment. In S.12 and S.15 she provides the tutor with another cue to
show that she has interpreted the assignment and is attempting to use her
interpretation. Thus far, the tutor's attention has not been on developing the
student's meaning but on his own distracting questions and comments.

The struggle for control is further developed in the following exchanges:

T.16: And who in your sense . . .

S.16: Very complex . . .

T.17: Pardon, the analysis of this response? I see. Who is your sense of the audience for this?

S.17: Very small. I basically write for most of the time for my class, my fellow students.

T.18: Who would you say is the first audience and who would you say is second audience?

S.18: Number one is the class and number two is the teacher.

T.19: That is quite a change from last term, isn't it?

S.19: Yes, because . . .

T.20: Can you sense the change when you write?

S.20: Of course, because when you write you have to be more formal. And if you write for the class it's much freer and easier style.

T.21: Not as much anxiety, doesn't cause as much anxiety?

S.21: No, not as much pressure.

T.22: So you have an easy, it sounds like you have an easier time getting your ideas down and worked out?

S.22: Right.

This passage, in which the tutor continues a series of questions unrelated to the issues that the student has raised, demonstrates the unfortunate effect of his habitual questioning pattern. The tutor and the student pursue independent tracks, forcing the student to assume the responsibility of avoiding distractions and keeping the conference on target. When the student observes that her task is "very complex," the tutor's formulaic response, "I see," implies comprehension, but nothing of the sort has been manifest in the tutor's interchanges with the student.

The exchange about the audience choice and lessened anxiety (T.17 through S.22) is built on the tutor's previous experience with the student when she could not write because of her extreme anxiety over a teacher's evaluation. However, the relationship of her previous anxiety to the lesson at hand is not articulated. What might the student have learned in this exchange thus far? No doubt, the student gets the message that the tutor's questions, not the student's meanings or interpretations, are of primary importance. The pedagogy practiced here is reminiscent of the traditional transmission model of teaching described by Paolo Freire in which the teacher asks the questions and the student attempts to answer or ignore them (1970, 58).

The next section of the dialogue demonstrates that the tutor again misses cues and delays the student's efforts to construct a meaningful text:

T.23: Okay, complicated little assignment, isn't it?

S.23: [Laughs]

T.24: Okay, how much time have you spent on this?

S.24: So far?

T.25: Yes.

S.25: Well, let's see. I did it on Sunday, so I spent about an hour writing the second draft and I took time.

T.26: And how much time studying it, researching it, and . . .

S.26: Research, I spent about one-half hour, I spent finding the book because it, the library in the art section, these kids take out books and they don't put them back in the right order on the shelf. And I couldn't find anything. And I spent about one-half hour finding the book, and say three-quarters hour reading it. There wasn't much on the artist. And, um, so I should say three-quarters of an hour. And I took an hour and a half to write the paper and on the second draft. About three hours on the assignment. Because it wasn't hard; it wasn't hard to respond, to write my response to it.

T.27: Um, so you started out by writing your response?

S.27: Yes, what I felt the painting meant.

T.28: Gives you a chance to, to put into your own words your analyses before you read someone else. Okay, what would be helpful for me to do when you read your paper?

The last entry of this exchange, T.28, is an important point at which to start. The tutor can claim to have acknowledged that the student's interpretation is important: "Gives you a chance to, to put into your own words your analyses before you read someone else. . . ." However, this advice has not been followed thus far through the session. For example, the tutor's first statement to the student, "Okay, complicated little assignment, isn't it?" devalues the student's efforts to tackle the assignment and to make sense of it. In effect, the authority of the tutor has dominated this in the same way that the critic's interpretation is often given priority by a reader of a text. The tutor continues to direct his questions away from the meaning of the assignment toward matters of secondary importance, such as the amount of time the student spent on research. Even when the student establishes that she has spent three hours with the assignment, the tutor neither acknowledges nor credits this effort. Why the tutor gathered this information is not explained to the student, nor is she complimented for demonstrating a high level of commitment to the assignment. What does the information gathered by the tutor tell him about the student's efforts to accomplish the assignment and her investment in the assignment? What does the tutor understand about the student's statement that the assignment was not hard nor the assignment hard to respond to (S.26)? Although the answers to these questions are difficult to determine, it seems clear that the purpose of the questioning, thus far, is to enable the tutor to gain control of the session. The tutor evinces no commitment to understanding the student's efforts to make a meaningful response to the assignment.

The final set of exchanges shows the continuing frustration of the student's efforts to get her tutor to assist her in elaborating her meaning:

> *S.28:* Um, I think it would be helpful if you, you get what I meant, what, if you get the gist of what I am trying to interpret out and if you think that I should mention, if you think I should mention any aspect of Ben Shahn's life that might relate to his painting. I don't know if I should mention that because I haven't mentioned about his lifestyle, or his childhood, or that he had a religious adaptation, or things like that. So, he did do quite a lot for children in America when he came here around the 1890s, and he found it strange that children didn't know what to do to read the Bible.

> *T.29:* He is from Russia?

> *S.29:* Russia.

> *T.30:* Okay, all right. So that means, basically, do I understand the meaning of your writing, of your ideas?

> *S.30:* He likes to write about social aspects, social human relations, and things like that.

> *T.31:* And so the question is, does that relate to your analysis of this painting? Is this his painting? *[pointing to the print]* "The Third Allegory"?

> *S.31:* To tell you the truth, when I first started with this painting, I wanted to know what I was doing so I checked the word, the perfect meaning of *allegory*. I came up with the, that it is supposed to be a symbolic representation of, of, you know, that would be meaningful to human beings. Yes, so I kept, I started to do this. I started to look for symbolic figures like the Ten Commandments, for example, so I started. Then I went onto the animal to make sure, a lion, a wolf, or something, or the fleece of a sheep and the legs look like a pig or a dog. I don't know, a disguise, you know, people do not always come to you as they appear to be. But, um, I, so I interpreted that as being bad people, and this is being good, this guy *[during this time she has*

been pointing to figures in the painting]. I said this guy was heralding the good news, that, um, good will finally overcome evil. And the
buildings in the back appear to be buildings, but if you look closely
you will see the crosses at the top. And they seem to be different
religions. I don't know.

T.32: So the figure of the animal, is being a deception?

S.32: A deception, right.

T.33: Um, the Ten Commandments, here, the man heralding the good news,
being the Ten Commandments and in the background you have, um,
steeples, actually.

S.33: Right. And I was also looking at the color coat. I don't know if that
has to do with Joseph.

T.34: Um, multicolored, because it certainly is there.

S.34: Yes, there is color and this is black-and-white.

T.35: Um.

S.35: I don't know if that is different races. He, he liked to do, you know, a
lot, you know, he liked to use a lot of colors. I think it could represent
the different races.

T.36: Um, why don't you go ahead and read the paper and we can talk
about it with respect to your analysis, why you gave the analysis,
reasons, and the, um, look at your research. Okay?

S.36: Research, where did I put it? Okay, I'll start.

Once again, the tutor initiates questions and comments (T.28, T.29, T.30,
and T.31) which the student either ignores or answers briefly. Despite these
interruptions, though, the student shows (S.28, S.30, and S.31) that she is
determined to continue her attempts to understand the painting and the relationship of the painter's life to the painting. Yet the tutor (T.29 and T.32)
does not respond to the efforts of the student to make sense of the painting.
His priority from lines T.28 through S.32 seems once again to be to maintain
control of the session by asking questions, rather than to engage the student
in a discussion of the ideas that she presents in almost every comment that
she makes.

In S.28, the student requests the tutor's help in two high-level areas. First,
she would like him to verify whether she has communicated what she intended ("I think it would be helpful if you . . . get the gist of what I am trying
to interpret"). Second, she would like his assistance in developing her intentions. Specifically, she needs strategies for integrating material about the
author's life into the text. The student has risen to the occasion; she could

not provide more powerful or more direct clues for the tutor to assist her in gaining authorship of her text.

At this point, this student needs to have the tutor step back, just as Paula Oye does in chapter 11, and permit the student to present and explore the plans that she has conceived for this piece of writing. The student appears to have a nascent vision of the shape that the essay might take. Often, even for the most skilled writers, such views fade quickly; she needs help in solidifying her view before it melts away. This is the critical moment of this conference; unfortunately, it is the student, not the tutor, who demonstrates the greater expertise, the better sense of what the writing task demands. She attempts to fill in the void created by the tutor's neglect of his responsibility. The tutor misses this opportunity that the student has created when he answers her request by asking a low-level factual question (T.29: "He is from Russia?") rather than by directly answering the student's requests. The tutor responds (T.30) only to the first part of the student's dual request; he ignores her request for strategies to integrate the information about the painter's life into the interpretation of the painting. The tutor's response is merely rhetorical and is not actualized. The student has been discussing (S.28 and S.31) her tentative interpretation of the painting and the possible relationships of the painter's life to this painting, but these topics are not further explored by the tutor. The student's attention is given both to the possibilities of the relationship of Shahn's life to meanings of the painting and to meanings of the painting built from the student's interpretation of symbolic representations. She ignores the tutor's question (T.31, "Is this his painting?") and continues on with her explanations. In actuality, the student is following the tutor's advice to develop her own response and interpretation (T.11 and T.28), but the tutor's efforts are directed toward maintaining control of the transaction, which, in effect, invalidates his advice. What is the student learning about the value of her ideas if the tutor does not directly attend to them or investigate them with the student?

In lines S.33 to S.35 there is a short exchange between the tutor and the student about the student's interpretation of the colors in the painting. However, this is ended after eight brief exchanges with the tutor's directive for the student to read her text, T.36. But the student has been *discussing* her text, forming her text, in an effort to develop her interpretation of the painting and her understanding of the relationship of the painter's life to the meanings of the painting. The text that the student brought with her is a draft which incorporates many of her responses to the tutor. During the conference, by means of her efforts to discuss her ideas with the tutor, the student was striving to develop her text.

Throughout these excerpts from the writing conference, the tutor's attention was given to the establishment of his authority through questions that consistently interfered with an adequate response to the material presented by the student. We have seen the tutor fail to grant the student ownership and authority of her ideas and developing text.

I would argue that to overcome deficiencies exhibited in this conference, we must respect students' authority as writers and grant them ownership of their texts. In chapter 8, Patrick Slattery shows that this task incorporates dual responsibilities: we must problematize or challenge students' thinking in order to keep them writing, and yet we must avoid telling them what, when, or why they are to write. Authority and ownership have been granted to the student writers when we:

1. Talk directly with writers about their ideas.
2. Discuss how we understand or misunderstand their ideas.
3. Explain our confusions and questions about what has been said.
4. Locate and identify strategies with the writers that continue their thinking and writing.
5. Present different points of view and perspectives that continue the writers' thinking and writing.

Through the analysis of writing conferences we can begin to recognize, acknowledge, and, where necessary, change the nature and intentions of our actions as teachers in order to help our students grow intellectually and gain independence as thinkers and writers.

Work Cited

Freire, Paolo. 1970. *Pedagogy of the Oppressed.* New York: Seabury Press.

III Cognitive Strategies: Engaging Students in the Activities of Expert Writers

Introduction to Section III

Thomas Flynn
Ohio University—Eastern

The interaction between novice and expert is often characterized by a sort of pushing and pulling or, as Patrick Slattery describes it in his essay in this section, supporting and challenging. Students often begin their university education with a writing strategy that has gotten them through their first twelve years of schooling, but that seems to have become a hindrance in their thirteenth year. Many students receive cues from their instructors that their writing skills are not adequate for the demands that they now face. Students are agonized by a desire to improve their skills and a reluctance to abandon practices that have benefited them. The resulting tension permeates all aspects of postsecondary writing instruction, including the relation between students and tutors. The students' need to economize effort and assess risk must be respected. Before turning their backs on their past strategies, students need to be shown the efficacy of new strategies. Students must be convinced that the effort that they put into mastering new skills will be appropriately rewarded because, as Giyoo Hatano and Kayoko Inagaki point out, understanding new processes requires much time and effort (1987, 36). The social setting of the writing conference, with its close interaction between novice and expert, is particularly well suited to this task.

The writing conference can provide an opportunity for cognitive apprenticeship, which is an especially powerful setting for learning because it incorporates the following features:

- learning is situated in a social context
- both novice and expert are active participants in the learning environment
- cognitive processes are externalized and displayed for inspection (Collins, Brown, and Newman 1989)

In this section the focus is on the cognitive processes that are being communicated by the tutor and acquired by the student. As studies of the differences between novices and experts demonstrate (Anderson 1987; Perkins and Salomon 1989; Voss 1989), experts build their competence on their knowledge of the domain, their knowledge of strategies appropriate to the domain, and their skill in applying their knowledge at the appropriate moment. The writing conference draws some of its strength from its ability to offer immediate feedback, which supports the students' skills and assists them in determining how best to make use of their skills. Novices need this assistance because oftentimes their knowledge is inert (Bransford et al. 1989; Whitehead 1929). Presented with appropriate clues, they can perform competently, but they do not know when to apply their skills. Thomas Schmitzer, writing in this section, presents an insightful description of how an expert can assist a student in activating knowledge that the student possesses but lacks the skills to use. Schmitzer describes a student who is relating his experiences of a trip through Europe but who is reluctant to break out of the chronological structure of the trip and make associations between those events and his political and historical observations. Schmitzer recognizes the limitations that the student is imposing on himself, and assists him in breaking through these limitations. The student wants to tell his experiences; Schmitzer encourages him to transform them.

Schmitzer is moving this student writer toward greater expertise. Signs of expertise manifest themselves differently in various domains, but in general as novices progress, they acquire greater knowledge, more strategies, and more skill in applying that knowledge appropriately. Dreyfus and Dreyfus suggest a useful outline of the steps that usually mark the progress toward expertise, the chief features of which are the following:

1. *Novice:* applies general strategies with little regard for context
2. *Advanced Beginner:* acquires more domain-specific strategies, which have been learned by applying general strategies in specific situations
3. *Competent Practitioner:* relies less on general strategies and more on appropriate selection of domain-specific strategies
4. *Proficient Practitioner:* goes beyond reliance on general strategies and begins to apply appropriate strategies without consciously analyzing and decomposing situations
5. *Expert:* demonstrates fluid performance, almost unconscious application of strategies, automaticity; possesses a large repertoire of situa-

tions that incorporate decision and action (1986, 16–50)

The goal in writing instruction is to move students toward expertise, to see them develop into advanced beginners and competent or proficient practitioners.

Each of the four essays in this section demonstrates how experts work with students to capitalize on the pedagogical richness of the writing conference. Thomas Schmitzer's essay, "Looking for Clues," describes how his conversation with a student about the phrase "streets lined with reminiscences" produced an instructional epiphany. The student's text dealt with his U.S. Air Force tour of duty in Europe, and in this writing the concept of *reminiscences* seemed for Schmitzer to intrude without warning. When he first mentioned the possibility of exploring the memories associated with those streets, the student was uncertain. His outline had no place for a digression into past associations. He had constructed a neat form that achieved directness by denying complexity; thus, he inadvertently gave his piece the two-dimensional flatness often noticed in the writing of novices. However, because of the social and cognitive dynamics of the conference, the writer and tutor were able to probe the significance of this phrase. As they investigated the phrase, a host of associations surfaced, and these connections, in turn, suggested a new, more complex and rewarding purpose for the student's text.

The tutor's expertise performed three key functions: it alerted the student to anomalies in his text; it encouraged him to take the risk of exploring these anomalies; and it supported him in the task of integrating newly discovered information into his essay.

Each of the other essays in this section shows experts researching and examining their practice of developing strategies that will give beginning writers increased control of their text and their writing process. At times, novices inadvertently distance themselves from the message that they would like to convey by relying on the limiting rhetorical patterns that they have used previously. Marcia Hurlow, Mary King, and Patrick Slattery all resist the students' attempts to achieve a simple solution to their rhetorical problems. The students' naive strategies neatly fit into Marlene Scardamalia and Carl Bereiter's description of the knowledge-telling approach to writing, while the experts' intervention in every case pushes the students toward a knowledge-transformation method of writing. Scardamalia and Bereiter point out the following essential traits of "knowledge telling":

1. Topical coherence: each sentence deals with the same broad topic, though each sentence may not connect with those around it
2. Superficially coherent structure
3. Topical homogenization: one rhetorical strategy (beginning, middle, end) is applied to all topics
4. Writing equated with recalling: the primary cognitive activity is recalling what occurred or recalling opinions
5. Minimal planning, goal setting, and problem solving
6. Limited revising (1986, 65)

When combined, these ingredients constitute a writing method that will enable the student to compose a limited response to any rhetorical demand. Understandably, students seem anxious about abandoning their practiced approaches because they are not yet fully convinced of the inadequacy of these approaches and because they do not know what can replace such approaches.

The psychological implications of this uncertainty that novices confront come across in Marcia Hurlow's essay, "Experts with Life, Novices with Writing." She recognizes that writing difficulties have ontological significance and that even when addressing matters seemingly as superficial as syntax, skilled tutors must consider their students' psychological as well as rhetorical resources. Her recognition of the sociocognitive aspect of the writing conference leads her to craft rhetorical practices that enable these writers to communicate more clearly and accurately the complexity of their thinking and experience.

Mary King and Patrick Slattery also direct their efforts toward constructing conferencing strategies that will enable writers to overcome independently the restrictions that hamper their writing. One serious barrier that impedes beginning writers is that they lack the specialized intellectual tools, the heuristics, that experienced writers can employ to serve the dual purpose of revealing the complex aspects of a topic and offering a rhetorical framework for expressing those insights. By equipping their students with these resources, both King and Slattery are moving their students away from the knowledge-telling strategy of novices to the knowledge-transforming strategy of experts, which is characterized by these features:

1. Skillfully managing cognitive behaviors associated with writing, such as generating ideas and editing

2. Searching memory in an organized manner, using heuristics to problematize writing tasks

3. Developing a mental image of the text to assist in reviewing and planning (Scardamalia and Bereiter 1986, 68)

The implications of choosing a knowledge-telling approach over a knowledge-transforming approach can be seen in Mary King's essay, "What Can Students Say about Poems? Reader Response in a Conference Setting," in which she gives an account of a student who has rejected the opportunity to take possession of a writing assignment to discuss Robert Frost's "The Silken Tent." Rather than run the risk of going beyond his perception of the teacher's implied constraints and creating meaning for himself, the student chooses to produce a text that is superficially coherent but at heart meaningless. The difficulties and choices that this writing assignment placed before this student are quite common. Frequently, students lack the skill and confidence to produce an authentic response that can both convey their experience with the poem and satisfy their instructor. To assist students in coping more successfully with literature-based writing assignments, King turns to reader-response criticism to develop a heuristic that will give students the assurance and the means needed to incorporate their own experience into their discussions of literary texts.

A similar dynamic works itself out in Patrick Slattery's essay, "Using Conferences to Help Students Write Multiple-Source Papers." He, too, recognizes that his students are stymied by the complexity of writing assignments. After reviewing intellectual development theory, Slattery develops a tutorial strategy that affirms students in their areas of competence by singling out their successful practices for support and that assists them in increasing their competence by challenging them to take the risk of trying new approaches.

The essays in this section capture the contributions that experts can make to the beginning writer's efforts to move beyond a limited repertoire of writing strategies toward a more sophisticated repertoire. They show teachers and students working together to assist the students in perceiving the intricacy of their writing tasks and in expressing that vision.

Works Cited

Anderson, John R. 1987. "Skill Acquisition: Compilation of Weak-Method Problem Solutions." *Psychological Review* 94:192–210.

Collins, Alan, John Seely Brown, and Susan E. Newman. 1989. "Cognitive Apprenticeship: Teaching the Craft of Reading, Writing, and Mathematics." In *Cognition and Instruction,* ed. Lauren B. Resnick. Hillsdale, N.J.: Lawrence Erlbaum.

Dreyfus, Hubert L., and Stuart E. Dreyfus, with Tom Athanasia. 1986. *Mind over Machine: The Power of Human Intuition and Expertise in the Era of the Computer.* New York: Free Press.

Hatano, Giyoo, and Kayoko Inagaki. 1987. "A Theory of Motivation for Comprehension and its Application to Mathematics Instruction." In *The Monitoring of School Mathematics: Background Papers,* vol. 2: *Implications from Psychology, Outcomes of Instruction,* ed. Thomas A. Romberg and Deborah M. Stewart, 27–66. Program Report no. 87-2. Madison: Wisconsin Center for Educational Research.

Perkins, D. N., and Gavriel Salomon. 1989. "Are Cognitive Skills Context-Bound?" *Educational Researcher* 18:16–25.

Scardamalia, Marlene, and Carl Bereiter. 1986. "Writing." In *Cognition and Instruction,* ed. Ronna F. Dillon and Robert J. Sternberg. Orlando, Fla.: Academic Press.

Voss, James. 1989. "Problem Solving and Educational Process." In *Foundations for a Psychology of Education,* ed. Alan Lesgold and Robert Glaser. Hillsdale, N.J.: Lawrence Erlbaum.

Whitehead, Alfred N. 1929. *The Aims of Education.* New York: Macmillan.

5 Looking for Clues

Thomas C. Schmitzer
Youngstown State University

One of the great advantages of one-to-one conferences in writing is that they present golden opportunities for seizing the teachable moment, that instance when a student feels the need to learn something new about the practice of writing. At such a time, the student is ready to transcend old habits, to develop new, more sophisticated writing strategies to replace the general strategies which until this time have served for all writing tasks. But even though the student is ready, support and guidance are needed to help the student develop, recognize, and practice the new strategy.

I have found that students want to make their writing more clear and significant for themselves and their readers, especially if the topic is something which matters to them. It often happens, however, that in the course of developing a subject, other ideas begin to obtrude themselves upon the narrative, ideas which sometimes do not relate to evolving sentences and paragraphs. To a novice, these appear to be simple intrusions, to be ignored or eliminated—but they may be clues to a new direction, fertile suggestions lying just beneath the consciousness of the writer.

Seasoned writers understand how to look for clues and how to develop these clues to their advantage. Student writers can be shown how to look for clues in their own writing or how to be on the alert for sudden switches in direction which may signal an impulse toward the creative. They can be taught to observe patterns in the text, recurring phrases or tendencies in related directions, which, while not directly pertaining to the subject of the composition, nevertheless may be clues to an arena of expression which the student had not consciously intended to enter.

An example of this type of growth occurred when a student from an advanced course in composition came to the Youngstown State University

An earlier version of this essay appeared in the conference proceedings of the East Central Writing Centers Association for 1985.

Writing Center to work on his writing independently of his coursework. He was interested in learning to develop his ideas, to give his writing a more interesting slant. He was ready to move beyond the familiar writing strategies which had carried him successfully to this point in his schooling, for he had achieved a level of intellectual development which now showed these strategies to be inadequate and limiting. After some discussion, we agreed that he should develop an essay on some topic that he was interested in recounting. He had recently returned from an extended tour in Germany, where he had served with the U.S. Air Force, and this experience had impressed him. He wanted to write about Germany, the wine, the culture, the Roman ruins that he had seen, and all of his experiences in that new environment.

In the course of developing this essay, the student produced a line that struck me as significant: "Before seeing the Black Gate," he wrote, "Rome *was* just a word in my vocabulary, but actually seeing this relic of Roman times gave a new definition to the word." The essay continued on after this announcement, left behind the Black Gate, and spoke now of travel-folder descriptions in which the student used the phrase "streets lined with reminiscences." I stopped at this phrase and asked what he meant by it. Although the paragraph appeared to have the conventional purpose of describing the German town of Trier, the student's discussion of the *reminiscences* and what he had intended by this word indicated that he had not left behind the Black Gate, nor the impressions that he had experienced when he wrote, "Rome *was* just a word in my vocabulary."

The student explained that the reminiscences which he had in mind were tied to high school history classes in which he had learned about Roman civilization. Recalling the streets of Trier, layered as they were with the sediments of past cultures, brought home to him the extent of the empire erected by the Caesars. This is what he had been thinking about when he wrote "streets lined with reminiscences." I suggested that he expand this phrase to better explain what he had intended; talking out his memories spurred him on, but he was worried that he might stray from the outline that he had drawn up to guide his writing. Outlining, a prewriting strategy taught to him in high school, had carried him this far, and the idea of violating this trusted practice created anxiety. Nevertheless, he went on working, but only with continual encouragement to do so. "Outlines are guides," I suggested, "not mandates."

I hoped that in exploring the intrusive idea, the student would discover the very kinds of material that he wanted in his writing: development of *ideas* rather than simple chronology, which would give his writing the more interesting start that he was after. After all, I reasoned, one skill that separates novice from expert writers is that of being able to distinguish tangents from fertile new directions. When students first begin to develop advanced writing skills, they tend to be cautious in deviating from their plans. Since their earlier writing was often rambling and loosely structured, once they develop some facility in organizing their ideas, they become fearful of deviating from their declared purpose. This caution results in conventional, predictable, lifeless prose. They reject more advanced, risky, and rewarding strategies, such as exploring alternatives that might either become dead ends or force them to restructure their conception of the writing assignment. Hubert Dreyfus and Stuart Dreyfus describe this as the advanced beginner stage (1986, 50). Novices have mastered a few strategies and apply them whether or not they are relevant. Novices need assistance in moving on to the level of competent practitioner, which will be marked by a more specific application of strategies and a greater ability to discern the barren from the fertile idea.

When my student finished unpacking the meaning hidden in his casual use of the term *reminiscences,* he had completed two pages of additional recollections and questions; he had extended the experience of his visit by recalling and reflecting on the intellectual experience. Now it became clear that the memories of the Roman Black Gate served to provoke questions concerning Roman "expansionist policy" and practices of "imperialism" which "intrude upon foreign soil." He further questioned in his writing why the Romans were not content with their own country and wealth, why they had to send soldiers abroad to occupy lands that were not their own. In short, probing his confrontations with a Roman ruin in a German town transformed the information that he recalled and led this former soldier, back from his stay in occupied Germany, to question governmental policies past and present.

Here were the rudimentary stirrings of a historic consciousness in the process of becoming aware of itself. Here, too, both student and instructor gained insight into the significance of looking for clues, as the student learned a new strategy for finding material in his draft on which to reflect, to create the significance and interest that he wanted his writing to display.

Work Cited

Dreyfus, Hubert L., and Stuart E. Dreyfus, with Tom Athanasia. 1986. *Mind over Machine: The Power of Human Intuition and Expertise in the Era of the Computer.* New York: Free Press.

6 Experts with Life, Novices with Writing

Marcia L. Hurlow
Asbury College

As more students over thirty years of age return to college, we are discovering more about their writing problems and processes, which in some aspects are distinct from those of the more traditional younger college students. Often older students are painfully aware of the difference between their writing abilities and those of expert writers, and seek the simplest, most risk-free means of reducing that difference. Many of these students, alarmed when they find themselves placed in a regular or an advanced composition class, question their instructors about whether they belong in a remedial class instead. They are often dubious when instructors explain that not only do college aptitude tests suggest that writing skills of high school students were better when these older students graduated than in recent years, but also that their more extensive life experiences will make them better writers.

During my study of syntactic development among freshman composition students, which was supported by a grant from the National Endowment for the Humanities, I found two major writing problems among writing students over thirty: choppy, syntactically oversimplified sentences, and rambling, inappropriately embedded sentences. Both problems seem to arise, in part, from the writer's insecurity about writing. In this essay I briefly describe two kinds of students whose insecurity is high and describe appropriate intervention strategies for solving their resulting writing problems.

Arnold H. Buss in his book *Self-Consciousness and Social Anxiety* (1980) explains that most adults outside of school do not frequently communicate at length in speech or writing and that most adults report fear of an audience. According to Buss:

An earlier version of this essay appeared in the conference proceedings of the East Central Writing Centers Association for 1985.

> The reported feelings of audience anxiety are similar to those of
> any strong fear: anguish, tension, and apprehension, which at times
> reach the intensity of panic and terror. There are two kinds of worry.
> One is simply *evaluation anxiety,* a fear of performing poorly and of
> failing. This fear of failure is common to all situations involving evalu-
> ation: a job interview, a test, or a school or work assignment . . .
> The second kind of worry is that of *being rejected as a person.*
> The speaker is concerned mainly about whether he will be liked and
> appreciated . . . The point here is that [an adult] is usually subject to
> two kinds of scrutiny by the audience. One kind, causing him to fo-
> cus on his performance, may cause evaluation anxiety. The second
> kind, causing him to focus on himself, may cause acute public self-
> awareness, a concern over his appearance or behavior. (167)

For older students, this anxiety-producing situation is often heightened
by the circumstances which brought them to college. As teenagers, students
may have thought that even high school was superfluous for the jobs that
they planned to have as adults. Only later do they realize that they need
additional training. My own older students have come to college under such
traumatic circumstances as being fired, divorced, widowed, or disabled both
physically and mentally and thus unable to perform the tasks of their previous employment; still another reason was converting to Christianity and being called to preach or to become a missionary. They come to school hoping
to facilitate or to resolve the situation in which they find themselves and
instead face further disquieting and disorienting obstacles in college.

Of course, not every nontraditional student will be anxious about writing,
and many of those who are will mask their anxiety to protect their self-
image, further complicating their writing problems:

> Like the Russian Matreshka dolls that nest neatly inside one an-
> other, students' intimate, imaginative feelings about what they . . .
> write remain hidden, covered by their larger, more public selves. There-
> fore, students' personal gifts, their singular ways of interpreting the
> world, go unnoticed by educators as the lines are drawn between pri-
> vate imaginative experiences and public academic expression.
> (Chiseri-Strater 1991, xvi–xvii)

Therefore, I developed an indirect elicitation test for insecurity and adminis-
tered it to a group of students. A theoretical explanation of the test appears
elsewhere (see Hurlow 1981). Then I examined the test results and samples

of writing from the over-thirty students. Samples of writing were taken from the students' freewriting journals and graded essays.

The freewriting journals were the pieces of writing closest to the students' unmonitored competence that I, as a teacher, was able to collect. Students knew that they were to write five pages a week in their journals, which would be graded on quantity alone, not on grammar, organization, diction, unity, or any other quality of writing. Although journals from this age group seldom had the very personal, diarylike qualities of the younger students, these writings generally were less reserved in tone and subject matter than their classroom essays, which I understood as indicating that evaluation anxiety was less intense in the freewriting journals.

To study students' self-monitoring, I examined their first graded compositions during that quarter and determined each sentence's T-unit, which "consists of a principal clause and any subordinate clause or nonclausal structure attached to or embedded in it" (O'Hare 1973, 10). I calculated the average length and syntactic complexity of sentences in both the essays and the journals. To determine the average length of the sentences, I counted the number and types of sentence embeddings from among the sixteen basic types in English. I also counted the number of embeddings which were ill-formed, by standard criteria.

Before sorting the students by age and gender, I correlated anxiety level with T-unit length and complexity and observed the following: First, students with higher insecurity had a longer average T-unit in their essays as compared to that in the journals. Second, students with higher insecurity used fewer clause types in their sentences. The correlation was smaller for the journals than for the essays. Third, pertaining to the correlation between average length of T-units and number of clause types: the T-units in the journals had a higher positive correlation with the number of clause types than those in the essays did.

Thus, there is a significant correlation between the number of clause types and number of words per T-unit and a student's linguistic insecurity. Further, the insecure students often have strikingly less sophisticated writing (by these syntactic measures) in essays for the teacher than in their journal entries. Linguistic insecurity also increased the difference between the journal and the essays in quality of syntactic structures, detail of examples, and general fluency. For most students, these aspects of writing are usually higher in the journals than in the essays, but the essays fall increasingly short in these qualities when the students are insecure. As their confidence builds, these qualities become more evident in their essays.

Nontraditional Female Students

As I added the students' age and gender to the correlations, more results emerged that matched the intuitions of many of my fellow composition teachers. First, among a high percentage of the older female students, the most common syntactic correlate of insecurity was choppy, repetitive, syntactically oversimplified sentences. Clauses were more often conjoined than subordinated. One of my colleagues recently came to me with the example below. He was baffled that an apparently intelligent woman, active in her community and church, would have written like this:

Starting Kindergarten

When my daughter started Kindergarten, I was really proud and also proud of her. I was proud last year when she went into Nursury School and especially proud when she had her graduation from Nursury School. But, I think I was most proud when she started Kindergarten, since Kindergarten, to me, seems like she is "growing up" because she is able to start school as well as being able to do a lot more on her own than she has ever been able to do before. This event took place about two weeks ago when I took her in to be registered at the Wilmore Elementary School here in Wilmore. It took place because it was time for her to start school since she was of age. I think that it shows a child is "growing up" when they can start school. I was proud because I was really happy and excited. . . .

Although this is the most repetitive example I have, it represents the qualities of syntax in my other case studies. This piece is also representative of older female writing students in that it exhibits evaluation anxiety. This student feels adequate as a person and, obviously, feels good about herself as a mother. However, in writing for her teacher, a kindly thirty-year-old man whose office is decorated with pages from his own young children's coloring books, she fears that her writing will not meet his expectations. She has simplified her thought in this short essay in order to "play safe" in the face of her teacher's evaluation.

In working with students experiencing evaluation anxiety, it is useful to begin with samples of the writers' unevaluated work and praise its strengths. After pointing out good qualities in the writing, it is fruitful to question the writers about the content in one or two of their short sentences, eliciting subordinated statements from the writers and having them write the new sentences, examining the relations between the parts. For this group of students in particular, grammar lessons, sentence combining, or other drills which focus on students' sentence-level deficiencies are often counterproductive, promoting continued distrust of their native competency and creating dependency on the teacher as an outside expert. Using sentence-combining techniques with the students' own work as the target sentences, however, can be useful.

I spend extra time with these women, talking about their lives. All older students need to know that their instructors respect them as adults and recognize the difference between them and the eighteen year olds in the same class. As we talk, I look for other areas of expertise in their lives which I have a personal need to understand. This personal link, which Paula Oye describes in chapter 11 as initially productive with her student Diane, is even more useful with older students, who have jobs, families, or other responsibilities and who can better identify with their instructors than with students of the more traditional college age. For example, the student may have children. I am a new mother, and my daughter has two teeth about to come in. My student could help me by writing an essay in answer to my questions: How did you make your children comfortable during this time? Did you use ointments? Is it useful to put teething rings in the refrigerator? Can you tell me about it in writing? By making the assignment more transactional and by creating a specific, knowable audience, the instructor allows the student to tap into his or her own expertise for a real purpose. As Susanna Horn demonstrates in chapter 10, students can most easily be helped by the strategy of first concentrating on content and then developing their linguistic competence, which will allow them to be part of the academic community. Confidence in the content of the writing also displaces, at least in part, the anxiety about the writing itself.

Using our relationship as a model for the writer's meeting the needs of a reader is also valuable to the writer's continued development, as David Bartholomae points out:

> Expert writers . . . can better imagine how a reader will respond to
> a text and can transform or restructure what they have to say around a
> goal shared with a reader. Teaching students to revise for readers,
> then, will better prepare them to write initially with a reader in mind.
> The success of this pedagogy depends on the degree to which a writer
> can imagine and conform to a reader's goals. (1985, 138–39)

Nontraditional Male Students

The second group of insecure nontraditional students was more narrowly defined statistically: male, upwardly mobile, and of middle or lower-middle socioeconomic status. These writers typically produced syntax that was rambling and inappropriately embedded. Such a student may try to fit his thought into a sentence pattern that the teacher has recently presented or that sounds to him like sophisticated writing. Seldom does this insecure student make a judgment about whether or not this kind of imitation is an appropriate method of choosing the best structure for conveying the thought. A more secure student is more likely to trust intuition, the native competence with language, for expression of the idea, with less concern for utilizing an "approved" structure.

A single example of this writing would be misleading, since the writers often take their cues from the conversation or the writing of professionals in their field of interest, although they are able to imitate it only imperfectly, relying heavily on jargon and a few stock phrases, most notoriously "at this point in time" and "in reference to [a particular topic]." For example, when I tried to explain to a student that he should not use the nominative form *I* as the object of a verb, he told me that he knew the rules, but that "Samuels will drive Thompson and I" sounded better at the office, and his boss wanted him to sound professional—it was important for his position with the organization. This student, like many others in the group, was less anxious about evaluation than about being rejected as a person. Instructors need to know, first of all, the place of communication in the workplace and our limits in teaching the most critical skills. As Lester Faigley points out:

> Even though the ability to write in certain discourses is highly valued in technologically advanced nations, power is exercised in a network of social relations and reconstituted in each act of communicating. No matter how well we teach our students, we cannot confer power as an essential quality of their makeup. (1989, 411)

These writers of inappropriately embedded sentences respond to the following approach. They need to explore other voices in the process of finding their own voice for writing. They also need to be assured of the tutor's respect. A good way to accomplish both is to ask the student to explain his job in such a way that the teacher could understand it. Keeping the topics focused on areas of the student's expertise while he develops more concise and precise prose helps him to keep from feeling rejected as a person. Talking about a proposed paper and even taping these conversations (if the stu-

dent is willing) for his later use can demonstrate to the student that he does
have ideas and words for expressing these ideas, as Thomas Schmitzer and
David Taylor explain in their chapters in this volume.

Overcoming Students' Insecurity

Older tutors of the same gender who have had similar experiences in return-
ing to college have been invaluable for these nontraditional students. Similarly, encouraging them to join a campus organization for older students (or
to form one, if none exist) can be extremely useful for helping these students
cope with problems that affect all of their college life, not only their insecurity in composition class.

Considering whether students' insecurity stems from fear of being evaluated or from fear of being rejected as a person makes it possible to design
appropriate approaches for particular students. More importantly, knowing
whether students' problems with writing stem from a lack of competence
with language or from an inability to tap fully into their competence because
of insecurity can make a difference in what is taught. Many errors will dis-
appear once writers feel secure enough to rely on their competence rather
than avoiding linguistic risks or trying to "sound correct" when what is correct is unclear to these writers.

Works Cited

Bartholomae, David. 1985. "Inventing the University." In *When a Writer Can't
Write: Studies in Writer's Block and Other Composing Problems,* ed. Mike
Rose, 134–65. New York: Guilford.

Buss, Arnold H. 1980. *Self-Consciousness and Social Anxiety.* San Francisco:
W. H. Freeman.

Chiseri-Strater, Elizabeth. 1991. *Academic Literacies: The Public and Private
Discourse of University Students.* Portsmouth, N.H.: Boynton/Cook.

Faigley, Lester. 1989. "Judging Writing, Judging Selves." *College Composition
and Communication* 40 (December): 395–412.

Hurlow, Marcia L. 1981. "Linguistic Insecurity and Syntactic Complexity." ERIC
Document Reproduction Service no. 203 314.

O'Hare, Frank. 1973. *Sentence Combining: Improving Student Writing without
Formal Grammar Instruction.* NCTE Research Report no. 15. Urbana, Ill.:
National Council of Teachers of English.

7 What Can Students Say about Poems? Reader Response in a Conference Setting

Mary King
University of Akron

Issues of classroom authority and responsibility have come to be perceived as presenting serious obstacles to students' intellectual growth. Composition teachers especially become aware of problems created for writers by the traditional pedagogy of teachers who have content expertise but who lack the skills to engage students in the mental activities of their disciplines. In the traditional view of schooling, authority has been accorded to the learned teacher, whose responsibility is simply to pass on his or her knowledge to students—not to develop in students the same skills that make the teacher an expert in his or her discipline. The students' responsibility is to commit the teacher's knowledge to memory. In the traditional literature classroom, the teacher's taste and aesthetic judgment comprise much of the knowledge for which the students are responsible.

Mike Rose relates a conversation with a professor which nicely illustrates the traditional mediating role of teachers. This professor arranged a conference with a student to rework the student's muddled paper on a Wordsworth poem. The professor reported, "I showed him line by line how the poem should be explicated. I figured he just didn't know, so I'd show him. But when he said back to me what I had said to him, I could see that we were talking completely past each other" (1990, 195).

They certainly were; the professor was asking the student to practice memory skills when the student needed to learn and practice the methods of literary inquiry used by expert readers of poetry—like his teacher. Rose observes that in keeping with his own training, the professor "saw his job as monitoring the rightness or wrongness of incursions into his discipline" (197). He did not imagine that it was his duty to engender in his students the

---

An earlier version of this essay appeared in the conference proceedings of the East Central Writing Centers Association for 1987.

domain-specific skills that he himself commanded, nor apparently did he have the expertise to do so.

Several concurrent developments in pedagogy and literary theory have made teachers aware that tradition allows the already skilled teacher to practice appreciation of literature but leaves the student mute, unpracticed, and still unskilled, able only to parrot (or try to guess) what the teacher thinks. Students have learned, in school, that they have nothing worthwhile to say about literature. After all, what can *students* say about poems? Students have to learn what the experts say, traditional thinking goes. What, in fact, students have to learn is expert strategies for finding things to say about poems. What students need is a radical departure from the traditional style of teaching literature. Reader-response theory provides a fruitful avenue to heuristics that will enable students to ask the sorts of questions that experts ask themselves when reading literature. Teaching that is based on reader-response theory can give students opportunities to practice their own responses to poems, to develop expertise rather than simply practicing memory skills.

Traditional teaching received a dramatic shock when Paolo Freire styled it as the banking concept of education, "in which the students are the depositories and the teacher is the depositor." In this view, "The more completely he fills the receptacles, the better a teacher he is. The more meekly the receptacles permit themselves to be filled, the better students they are" (1970, 58). Freire's derisive comments took aim at the Brazilian education system as a support for the socioeconomic power structure. That view made similar educational practices in the United States look antidemocratic and outmoded, augmenting the impact of new pedagogies, such as Kenneth Bruffee's Brooklyn Plan, which are based on the social construction of knowledge—the idea that human beings create knowledge in the process of communicating with each other. Increasingly, students in writing classes work in groups, discussing each other's ideas and drafts—taking responsibility and authority for understanding and improving their own and each other's texts. The teacher has become less prominent as a source of knowledge.

Coming together with these shifts in political perception and pedagogical practice was a shift in the focus of literary criticism from the text to its effects on readers—reader-response criticism. Like its predecessors, reader-response criticism is concerned with establishing meaning for literary works. In fact, says Jane Tompkins, "All modern criticism . . . takes meaning to be the object of critical investigation, for unlike the ancients we equate language not with action but with signification" (1980, 203).

An understanding of just how readers create significance in relation to literary text is a matter of great importance for teachers as well as for literary critics, and much has been written on this subject. Louise Rosenblatt is one of the earliest and most accessible writers on reader response; Tompkins says that Rosenblatt is "first among the present generation of critics in this country to describe empirically the way the reader's reactions to a poem are responsible for any subsequent interpretation of it. . . . Her work . . . raises issues central to the debates that have arisen since" (xxvi). Rosenblatt is thus of interest to the student of response theory; *The Reader, the Text, and the Poem* (1978) is directly useful to teachers as well because in it Rosenblatt lays groundwork for heuristics which enable students to respond in writing as they read, writing which will constitute a record of their reading activities and a basis for further, more formal writing on assigned topics. Teaching such strategies, whereby novice readers can attach meaning to poems, places responsibility on students and allows them to practice some of the skills that expert readers call into play when reading literary works of art, to "find clues . . . to the complex ties between literacy and culture" (Rose 1990, 8). By using such strategies, students can find plenty to say about poems.

Students learn to attend to the text under study when teachers give them authority to write their own responses. But if teachers impose too many constraints, students become increasingly alienated from their own responses, and their writing is emptied of meaning. I want to show an extreme example of such writing and then show how students can be directed through a writing process that trains them to read literature aesthetically and independently. This process can help students maintain authorship of the paper that must be written, even when the topic is closely controlled.

Below is a writing sample brought into the Writing Center by a second-semester composition student. He was actually a very good writer during his first semester, when he was doing personal writing in his composition class. He had been a bit overschooled at a serious college prep boarding school and had to learn how to trust his own voice, but he was capable of very creative and interesting writing. I will call him Biff, in honor of his prep background. He enjoys reading poetry and responds strongly to it, but look at the opening of his draft on Frost's poem "The Silken Tent."

Syntax and Diction Complement the
Theme of Frost's "The Silken Tent"

In order to make a complete peanut-butter and jelly sandwich, the two main ingredients peanut-butter and jelly must be applied to two

pieces of bread. The theme of a poem is similar to the two part requirements for a complete sandwich, in that it also requires two elements. The two elements are syntax and diction. The theme cannot be
complete without the proper application of these elements. Their effective usage must be displayed within a poem for the theme to be
fully expressed to the reader. The theme of Robert Frost's poem, "The
Silken Tent," is masterfully complemented by his usage of syntax
and diction throughout his entire poem.

What on earth is Biff doing? Well, he is fulfilling his assignment. The
assignmment required that he do three things: study an essay written by his
teacher on *theme* in literature; read what two critics of his choice said about
"The Silken Tent"; and then write a paper explaining how syntax and diction complement the theme of the poem. Though Biff dutifully gathered
information and spent hours composing the paper, the task was not his task
and the paper never became his paper. He repeated his assignment in his
introduction, only inflating it with a goodly amount of hot air: "The theme
of Robert Frost's poem, 'The Silken Tent,' is masterfully complemented by
his usage of syntax and diction throughout the entire poem." In fact, that
sentence is Biff's thesis—or rather, his teacher's thesis. I asked whether
complemented was really the word he wanted, and he nodded with the confidence that comes with complete closure. I read him a dictionary definition,
and he still nodded confidently. Finally, I asked why he had used *complemented,* and he said: "That was in our assignment. That's what she wanted."
The analogy of the peanut butter sandwich was also something that his teacher
would want, because "she likes analogies." So this literally was not Biff's
paper. He did as he was told, strove valiantly, and produced an awful paper.
It was impossible to deflect him from his path when he came into the writing
center, because his writing had reached an advanced stage on an assignment
which had taken the poem away from him and put other texts in its place:
the teacher's discussion of theme, the two critics' analyses of the poem, and
the direction to look at syntax and diction, terms which he did not grasp
firmly.

Had Biff come to the center earlier in his writing process, we could have
delayed tackling the assignment. Since he was not sure what to do, he relied
on the general, weak strategies that had gotten him this far in school, such as
figuring out "what the teacher wants" and doing it; and using the assignment
as a thesis. Instead, we first would have given the poem to him by having
him do some prewriting tasks designed to help him, as Mike Rose says,
"find knowledge that the assignment didn't tap" (1990, 8), strategies such as

those that experts use to produce their ideas about poetry. Then he would be able to assume ownership of the paper as well. To develop such tasks, I want to turn now to Rosenblatt's view of readers, texts, and poems.

Rosenblatt assigns a role to the reader that requires both considerable activity and keen awareness of that activity. The text is a set of verbal symbols, which functions as a stimulus to the reader's imagination and as a blueprint to guide the reader's attention throughout the reading experience. *The poem*, then, is Rosenblatt's term for the reader's experience with the text of a literary work of art. I will use *the poem* that way too, as shorthand for the reader's transaction with any work of drama, fiction, or poetry.

The poem is created in this way: "The reader actively builds up a poem for himself out of his responses to the text, drawing on past experiences, both external reference and internal response, that have become linked with the verbal symbols; relating referents and reinterpreting as he goes along, not having actually read the first line until he has read the last; and fusing ideas with feelings, associations, and attitudes that have been called forth" (Rosenblatt 1978, 10). So there is no tangible object that is the poem—there is only a text which elicits responses from the reader in an aesthetic transaction which is the poem.

Rosenblatt focuses the majority of her attention on the reader, and so should teachers, in order to set their students on the route from novice to expert readers of poetry, for, says Rosenblatt, "built into the raw material of the literary process itself is the particular world of the reader" (11), which the teacher can teach the reader to discover. Many students have never taken this active role in their reading. They haven't been taught how, and many have never discovered for themselves how to engage in any aesthetic transaction with a text.

Moreover, conflicting with the reader's ability to engage in this aesthetic transaction is the more common and directly useful reading that we practice in our daily lives, both in and out of school. Good students like Biff already possess expertise in this domain. During nonaesthetic reading, the reader responds to the text as symbols of "concepts to be attained, ideas to be tested, actions to be performed after the reading," such as directions, material to be studied for a test—and literature to be analyzed in order to write a paper. The reader's attention is directed outward, "focused primarily on what will remain as the residue after the reading" (23). Biff's teacher was directing his attention outward with her assignment, and Biff responded by reading nonaesthetically, industriously rummaging in "The Silken Tent" for syntax and diction.

What the skilled nonaesthetic reader does not know, and may learn only with difficulty, is how to respond aesthetically, how to attend to "what happens during the actual reading event . . . [how to attend to] the associations, feelings, attitudes, and ideas that these words arouse within him . . . [how the reader centers attention] directly on what he is living through during his relationship with that particular text" (23–24).

Notice how emphatically Rosenblatt gives ownership of the aesthetic experience to the reader. But many student readers are so encumbered, so heavily laden with the purposes of their teachers as they read, that they have very little chance of finding their own responses to the text. They somehow would have to bypass or overcome their habitual nonaesthetic stance in order to experience the poem. But teaching can be done in such a way as to give students the skills to read their poem and to write their own paper—not the teacher's.

The best way of giving the poem to students is for students to write about it before they have completed their reading, to record impressions and experiences which they can later contrast with the experience gained after they have read the entire piece. When students have written to their own satisfaction, ask them to continue writing briefly, describing their own feelings about what they have read up to this point. Students often find that they are novices at the task of conveying their feelings about the poem—they have never been asked to do so before. In fact, their prior experiences with reading literature in school have generally shown them that they are incapable of finding what they often refer to as "the hidden meaning"—that meaning which the teacher reveals. So writing their own responses gives students an opportunity to practice, to rehearse statements that they might want to make about the poem. After each bit of writing, ask students to read aloud what they have written. Such reading aloud gives writers time to contemplate what they have said and perhaps to add new thoughts. It also lends dignity to the rough beginnings of students' entry into conversations about literature, as the teacher emphasizes the value of their efforts.

In the past, I was uncertain of what to do if a student had not read the work of literature. Sometimes I simply told the student to use the writing conference to complete the reading. This authoritarian behavior went counter to good writing center pedagogy, but I believed it when I said, "We can't do anything until you've read the poem." Now I know that the most fruitful beginning can be made right at the first stage, and I wish all students would come in at this ideal time.

It is important to sharpen the student's attention in the early stages of the reading process, because it is at this the stage that the reader can experience the poem as an event by observing the personal response evoked by the text. To do so, says Rosenblatt, "the reader who seeks to participate in a poem or novel or play must face ultimately a unique task of selection, synthesis, and interpretation. . . . In the reading of a literary work of art, this activity is raised to the level of creative adventure. In this sense, the 'shaping spirit,' the 'synthetic and magical power' of the imagination, which Coleridge attributed to the poet, can also be claimed for the reader" (52). If the student is to claim this power as a reader, he or she needs permission to engage in a process of responding to the features of the text that generate "the reader's need to live through to some resolution of tensions, questions, curiosity or conflicts aroused by the text, [a need which] gives impetus to the organizing activity of the reader" (54–55). In order not to interfere with this organizing activity, it is better to assign general tasks which call forth readers' own responses, rather than specific writing tasks.

Emphasize that these writing tasks are prewriting activities—students are not at this point "writing the paper," that is, producing texts that will be handed in, or even drafts of their ultimate texts. Rather, students are exploring their own experience, creating a personal poem which will then be available for examination. They are not writing the paper, but what they write will become the basis for the paper. For this creative activity, freewriting is the most fruitful method; if a student does not know how to use freewriting, here is a prime opportunity to show how helpful freewriting can be in the early stages of composing. The student who wants to begin by writing the first sentence of the paper is now faced with an assignment so complex that he or she cannot do it that way. The student may be ready to learn a more complex process which delays the writing of the actual paper and instead permits the writer to assume a stance in relation to the literary work of art about which he or she must write. After all, how can the student produce a clear thesis from a tabula rasa—the blank that his or her mind produces when faced with the writing task at hand?

Text as Stimulus

Here are some questions for prewriting that prompt readers to address the text as stimulus. They are a useful heuristic at any stage of reading and are especially useful for focusing the readers' attention when they have read only part way through the text.

1. *What can readers understand or react to in the text?* At first, when students have read some of a text, simply ask them to write about their impressions of the text. Then ask them to write for five more minutes giving an opinion about the speaker or the characters and events. If students can explore in this way before completing the reading, they often say that writing about the first part helped them "pay attention during the rest of the story." But even if students have finished reading the piece, this task is still useful because it takes readers back into the text.

2. *What memories, thoughts, or feelings does the text evoke?* Answering this question is fruitful even if students understand very little, as might at first be the case with a verbally complex text, such as *Oedipus Rex* or Melville's "Bartleby, the Scrivener." The act of writing helps begin the transaction in which the poem is created. This activity may overlap the following question; that is, readers may spontaneously return to peruse the text and focus on its most salient or powerful elements.

3. *What is important to the readers in the experience of the text?* This writing activity turns the students' attention to the text once again, helping them internalize the text. This is the beginning of engagement.

Text as Blueprint

Next, as blueprint for the reading experience, help students explore the poem in the following way:

1. *What seems most important at first? How does that change?* During the process of reading, students order and correct their responses: the poem is a new experience which they cannot know until they have been through the entire poem. These questions help readers become aware of the emerging coherence that they build in their search for consistent interpretation of the experience. Readers are drawn back to the text to account for their shifts in attention and to trace the growth of their sense of the significance of what they have read. This activity may lead into the next without prompting.

2. *What is my experience with the text? How can I characterize it? What can I point to in the text to support what I am saying about it?* This set of questions constitutes a kind of generic assignment for writing about literature. After students have written responses to all the questions,

they often recognize how their writing provides material and direction to fulfill the assignment. Even Biff's topic can now be seen as no more than a variant of this prewriting heuristic, altered as follows to accommodate the terms of the assignment: What are the experiences of the two critics that I have read? What examples of syntax and diction can I point to in the text to support what my teacher says in her essay about theme in literature?

Encouraging Student Ownership of the Text

If Biff had viewed his assignment in terms of the above set of questions, he might have been able to write a more substantive paper and one which was more academically respectable as well, for, writing from this perspective, he would attribute to the appropriate authors the points of view that he incorporated in his essay, rather than treating these assertions as truth. He would have identified the various voices which speak in his essay as merely those of other human beings whose ideas he was bringing together. Students who can do this may be able to free themselves from what David Bleich calls "the academic psychology of social detachment" (1988, 17), which requires ignoring the social and collective basis of language and knowledge. Biff would then have had a chance to escape the parodic quality of his topic sentence ("The theme of Robert Frost's poem, 'The Silken Tent,' is masterfully complemented by his usage of syntax and diction"), which is in part an aspect of his knowledge-telling approach to writing—simply stringing together the pieces of information that the assignment supplied. (For a description of a knowledge-telling approach to writing, see pp. 55–56 in the introduction to section three.)

But since Biff viewed knowledge about the poem as external to himself—located in the teacher and in the other texts that he read—he felt that he had neither the responsibility nor the authority to transform it. Biff was rather like Marcia Hurlow's older students (described in chapter 6), obsessed with pleasing authority figures rather than making meaning. And in fact, Biff showed only a very superficial familiarity with the poem itself—the ostensible subject of his paper—and attached far more significance to the critical essays that he had read. The poem, then, disappeared as a text, and as an event, in Rosenblatt's terms, it simply never took place.

The most crucial moments in a writing conference devoted to literature occur in the first stages when the teacher encourages the student to experience the text as stimulus and as blueprint by writing responses to the heuristic questions. If the process is successful, students own the poem, for they have created it themselves. And they are now ready to tackle the assignment—even an assignment such as Biff's.

An instructional process which continually affirms students' right to engage in aesthetic reading of literature expands almost infinitely as students move through the various poems presented in a course, practicing free responses and focusing on what is important to them in work after work. A single writing conference will not supply the skills withheld during years of traditional teaching, when texts were presented only to be interpreted by the teacher. Rosenblatt puts the case clearly when she declares, "Someone else can read a newspaper or a scientific text for you and paraphrase it quite acceptably. But no one can read a poem for you. . . . Accepting an account of someone else's reading or experience of a poem is analogous to seeking nourishment through having someone else eat your dinner for you and recite the menu" (1978, 86). Yet well-meaning teachers like the professor whom Mike Rose describes do present their own readings, thinking that they are modeling the reading act. Perhaps they do not suspect that instead they are taking over the privilege of reading the poem. Perhaps they are not consciously depriving their students of the opportunities that readers need in order to develop the skills of concentration and attention, the capacity to hold in mind many memories of the text, of other texts, of life experiences, "to live fully and personally in literary transaction" (Rose 1990, 161).

But teachers who present their own readings as authoritative *are* depriving their students. Novices need opportunities to practice reader response, to engage in that internal dialogue which creates a connection between the reader and the text, establishing a version of meaning in the form of a reader-based text and providing the foundation for external dialogue. "From this could flow growth in all the resources needed for transactions with increasingly demanding and increasingly rewarding texts" (161). Such growth takes place as students become engaged in the text—they remember their own lives, they grant true importance to their feelings, and they come to recognize the immense value of art in helping people learn what it means to be more fully human by practicing the uniquely human social behavior of talking about literature.

Reader response provides the kind of pedagogy that Rose says is needed, one that "encourages us to step back and consider the threat of the standard classroom and that shows us, having stepped back, how to step forward to invite a student across the boundaries of that powerful room" (238). Using reader response, we can make "that powerful room" hospitable, offering responsibility and authority to all the members of the group rather than hoarding the power and expertise among ourselves.

Works Cited

Bleich, David. 1988. *The Double Perspective: Language, Literacy, and Social Relations.* New York: Oxford University Press.

Freire, Paolo. 1970. *Pedagogy of the Oppressed.* Translated by Myra Bergman Ramos. New York: Seabury Press.

Rose, Mike. 1990. *Lives on the Boundary: A Moving Account of the Struggles and Achievements of America's Educational Underclass.* New York: Penguin Books.

Rosenblatt, Louise M. 1978. *The Reader, the Text, the Poem: The Transactional Theory of the Literary Work.* Carbondale, Ill.: Southern Illinois University Press.

Tompkins, Jane. 1980. *Reader-Response Criticism: From Formalism to Post-Structuralism.* Baltimore: Johns Hopkins University Press.

8 Using Conferences to Help Students Write Multiple-Source Papers

Patrick J. Slattery
University of Arkansas

Many assignments in college require students to write about complex topics with which they have little or no firsthand knowledge; therefore, many teachers ask their students to use multiple sources of information to write about these topics. We are probably all familiar with the kinds of problems that students can have with this type of writing—many students, for instance, initially have trouble with the skills of summarizing, paraphrasing, quoting, and citing sources. In my experience, however, students writing from multiple sources have had more difficulty with analyzing divergent viewpoints and with staking out and justifying their own positions. In the introductory essay in this collection (chapter 1), Thomas Flynn argues that recent work in cognitive science has begun to establish conferencing as one of the most effective methods for instructing students in higher-order thinking skills. Drawing from cognitive psychology, I apply intellectual development theory to composition in order to illustrate how we can use conferences to help students think more critically about the contradictory perspectives reflected in their sources.

Representative Student Papers

First I want to summarize three student papers that suggest the types of problems that my students tend to have when they write from sources. Written for a freshman composition course on multiple-source writing, each of these papers focused on a complex topic and brought to bear on that topic several magazine, newspaper, and journal articles.

An earlier version of this essay appeared in the conference proceedings of the East Central Writing Centers Association for 1987 and in *College Composition and Communication* 41 (1990): 54–65.

Paper 1

The author of a paper titled "Using Animals for Laboratory Testing" recognized that scientists and antivivisectionists disagree about the use of lab animals in research, explaining that many people feel that animals should not be used for testing because it is cruel, whereas "others feel that they must be used in order to make medical advances." According to the paper, however, this diversity of opinion is not really legitimate. "Medical advancements have benefited the members of the antivivisectionist groups," the student wrote. "Don't they realize this? When taking an aspirin tablet or a bite of prepackaged food, the members of those groups should realize that a laboratory animal had to try it first!" To justify his position in favor of animal research, the student presented the view of a high school teacher whom I will call Mr. G: "Mr. G, religion teacher at Memorial High School, says, 'These tests are performed. . . . The Bible tells us that animals were put forth on earth by God in order to serve man.'" After summarizing Mr. G's point of view, the student modeled his own position exactly on the point of view of this authority, concluding, "We must follow some sort of ethical code. . . . I believe that vivisection is ethically and morally right. I believe that animals were put forth on earth by God to serve man."

Paper 2

The author of the second paper, "Soap Operas: How They Are Affecting Viewers," realized that some authorities believe that watching soaps is detrimental, while others think it is beneficial. She explained that one expert argues that teenagers tend to "misjudge the amount of sex between unmarried partners and married partners" and "to overestimate significantly the number of unfaithful spouses, divorces, illegitimate children and abortions in the real world." Furthermore, according to this paper, some experts believe that even adults have trouble distinguishing reality from fantasy: once, when a character was kidnapped on a daytime soap, an older viewer "placed a long distance telephone call to the network station and told them where they could find the missing character." "On the other hand," the student wrote, "some studies have shown it may be beneficial to watch soaps." She noted that one authority believes that "teens who watch soaps tend to take fewer drugs because the soaps serve as the same kind of an escape as drugs do" and that some adults "may even be prescribed to watch a soap opera if there is a character dealing with the same problem the patient is." This student offered a balanced picture of the topic, concluding, "All in all, whether you should watch soap operas or not seems left up to your own judgment. I think it all depends on your own view of soap operas."

Paper 3

The author of a third paper, "Terrorism: Protecting U.S. Embassies and Diplomats," evaluated solutions set forth by three experts—increased security, better intelligence, and military retaliation. The student wrote that if security included "less glass and fewer windows, blast-resistant walls, and better electronic monitoring systems," embassies will be "better able to resist substantial damage from terrorist attacks." Considering the second solution, better intelligence, the student explained that "as information about a planned terrorist attack is obtained, the U.S. can activate such preventive strikes as arresting terrorists before they can attack or moving military forces to the threatened area." But he admitted that "although increased intelligence reduces the number of attacks . . . it cannot curtail the effects of terrorist attacks when they do happen." After evaluating these two proposed solutions, the student asserted, "Increased intelligence must be used in conjunction with better security." Turning to the last solution, military retaliation, the student pointed out that some officials, many of whom believe that "idle threats create the impression that America is impotent," argue that military force is the best solution, but he also noted that "some experts on terrorism believe that actual retaliation will . . . fuel anti-Americanism, thus resulting in even more terrorist attacks against U.S. embassies." Responding to these two viewpoints, the student argued that because "the risks in using and threatening to use retaliation are too high . . . retaliation should not be included in Washington's plan to better defend U.S. embassies abroad."

Intellectual Development Theory

I suspect that many composition teachers can recognize in these examples some of the ways in which their students approach multiple perspectives; nevertheless, it is difficult to account for these differences. Surely, the less appropriate approaches are in part due to the students' lack of experience with writing college-level essays. But I find especially provocative another kind of account—the possibility that differences in students' writing are related to intellectual orientations that develop during college.

According to William Perry, as students attend college, their implicit metaphysical and epistemological assumptions grow increasingly complex. In *Forms of Intellectual and Ethical Development in the College Years: A*

Scheme (1970), Perry suggests that students who filter their educational experiences through what he calls a "dualistic" intellectual framework accommodate diversity in terms of "right" and "wrong." Such students might not believe that they have access to knowledge about reality, but they assume that legitimate authorities do. Confronting divergent viewpoints in black-and-white terms, these students dogmatically accept the view of the "right" expert and unreflectively reject the perspective of the "wrong" one. Students who construe experience from a "multiplistic" intellectual orientation, however, have different metaphysical and epistemological assumptions. These students, who realize that even reliable authorities do not know everything, might implicitly assume that objective reality exists, but they do not believe that it can be known with any certainty. And since these students understand that even a legitimate authority does not have access to absolute knowledge, they assume that divergent points of view must be equally valid. Finally, students who approach contradictory opinions from a "relativistic" intellectual stance realize that despite the inherent ambiguity of knowledge, some argumentative positions approximate reality better than others. These students accept the fact that an authority cannot know reality with certainty, and yet they compare and evaluate alternative opinions, making judgments about which ones are more rational or better supported.

Perry's model of intellectual development seems to account for some of the differences in the three student papers, but his scheme can be problematic because his research base was limited to male undergraduates at Harvard. Patricia Bizzell argues that Perry's model is culture-specific, pointing out that we are teaching students "to think in a certain way, to become adults with a certain kind of relation to their culture, from among the range of relations that are possible." "In short," sums up Bizzell, "Perry provides us with a useful picture of the kind of 'cultural literacy' required in a liberal arts college" (1984, 452–53). Adding that Perry's scheme could be gender-biased, Blythe Clinchy and Claire Zimmerman test it against a sample of undergraduate women. They conclude that the model on which they base their research with women "is largely a fuller and more precise articulation of Perry's" (1982, 163), but they also point out some differences between Perry's students and their own. For example, when the women in Clinchy and Zimmerman's study approached diversity from a relativistic framework, they seemed to do so with a different attitude than the men in Perry's study. According to Clinchy and Zimmerman, "the men sounded aggressive; they used contextual reasoning to attack problems. The women sound receptive. They say that in analyzing a text they must leave their own minds behind and enter the author's mind" (173). In *Women's Ways of Knowing: The Development of Self, Voice, and Mind* (1986), Mary Field Belenky et al. refer to these differences in relativistic thought as "separate" and "connected" ways of knowing.

Furthermore, Perry's scheme can lull teachers into reducing differences in thinking to a series of sequential positions, a reduction that can lead to pigeonholing certain types of students into particular stages. For example, Janice Hays describes a research project for which she asked freshmen to write on either abortion or marijuana and to pretend in their essays that they were speaking on a panel composed of representatives from community organizations. Evaluating these student papers, Hays asserts that the basic writer argues dogmatically without analyzing different points of view, that the basic writer "perceives a multiplicity of perspectives as alien intruders into a dualistic universe" (1983, 133). I would argue that Perry's model is valuable not so much because it explains distinct stages through which all people systematically pass, but rather because it suggests a strategy for conferencing with college students.

Implications for Conferencing

Developmentalists suggest that teachers can foster intellectual growth most effectively by simultaneously supporting students in terms of how they currently think and challenging them to think in slightly more complex ways. Students need to be challenged, since it is by confronting experiences that they cannot cognitively process that they develop more complex thinking constructs. Without sufficient support, however, the painful and risky process of intellectual growth can overwhelm students, perhaps even forcing them to retreat to a less complex orientation (Widick and Simpson 1978). The developmental view suggests, then, that to promote intellectual growth, a teacher would respond individually to students' thinking, both supporting and challenging the orientation reflected in each paper written by every student. This view seems appropriate for writing tutors because, as Thomas Flynn argues in chapter 1, structured interaction between novice and expert is the crux of conferencing.

Paper 1

To respond to the first paper, "Using Animals for Laboratory Testing," a tutor could support the writer's current dualistic orientation and also challenge him to view and write about animal experimentation more multiplistically. A support response could praise the student's introductory summary of scientists' and antivivisectionists' perspectives. A challenge response could encourage the student to realize that this diversity of opinion is epistemologically legitimate. My challenge responses usually take the form of questions, but as JoAnn Johnson suggests in chapter 3, questions can sometimes alienate students. For example, to ask the writer of the first essay to confront the writing task relativistically might initially overwhelm him, perhaps even leading to a deeper entrenchment in dualism. Specific support and challenge responses for the paper on animal experimentation might sound like the following:

> *Support Response:* In the beginning of your paper, you do a good job of summarizing the viewpoints that scientists and antivivisectionists have on animal experimentation. The topic is complex because both groups have some legitimate claims.

> *Challenge Response:* Explain your reasons for rejecting the antivivisectionist view and for accepting the scientists' perspective. Can you imagine a situation in which it would not be ethically sound or scientifically valid to conduct experiments on animals? Can you identify the assumptions of any of the experts to whom you refer? What might be the particular biases of a religion teacher, a scientist, and a member of the animal rights coalition? Do you have any biases concerning this topic?

Paper 2

To respond to the second paper, "Soap Operas: How They Are Affecting Viewers," a tutor could support the student's multiplistic understanding of soap operas but then challenge her to approach the topic more relativistically—that is, to recognize the relative worth of divergent perspectives. A support response might commend the student's openness to the experts' contradictory opinions. A challenge response could encourage her to structure the essay in a way that lends itself to analyzing and evaluating these viewpoints. A tutor might use comments such as the following to talk about the second student paper:

> *Support Response:* In researching your topic, you've found that experts disagree about the effects that soap operas have on viewers, and in your paper you summarize the authorities' perspectives accurately and fairly.

Challenge Response: You structure your paper around the negative and positive effects of soap operas, first presenting the negative effects that some researchers say soap operas have on teenagers and adults, and then presenting the positive effects that other researchers say soaps have on these same age groups. To compare the experts' contradictory opinions, you might try organizing your essay around the two age groups rather than around different types of effects. Consider the potential positive and negative effects of watching soaps on one age group at a time—teenagers, for instance—and analyze the divergent views. What types of research, evidence, and reasoning do the experts provide? Do some conclusions seem more valid than others?

Paper 3

The comments suggested for the first two papers are designed to promote growth to a slightly higher position on the scheme of intellectual development. However, because the author of the third essay, "Terrorism: Protecting U.S. Embassies and Diplomats," already seems to think and write reflectively about his topic, this goal seems inappropriate for a conference about his paper. In responding to this paper, a tutor could commend the student for thinking relativistically about terrorism and then challenge him to think just as critically about other topics. Although teachers can direct challenge responses toward past essay assignments, if a student is beginning to research a new topic, as was this writer, I try to focus challenge responses on the new task. A support response for the paper on terrorism could point out to the student that he successfully evaluates the proposals for beefing up security, increasing intelligence, and military retaliation, and in the process he reaches a reasonable judgment about the solutions. A challenge response could encourage him to approach his new topic of world hunger similarly. A tutor's responses to the third paper might sound like the following:

Support Response: You evaluate the experts' proposals well. By analyzing each solution's strengths and weaknesses, you persuasively argue for a combination of increased security and improved intelligence. Furthermore, although you decide against using military retaliation, you consider an opinion in favor of this solution and seem to understand the reasoning behind it.

Challenge Response: When you begin drafting your essay on U.S. responses to world hunger, try to analyze your new subject as you have this topic, weighing the strengths and weaknesses of different proposals. What have been the successes and failures of U.S. attempts to abate world hunger? What are the political, social, and economic contexts from which the different programs have emerged? After evaluating past attempts to curb hunger, see if you can make any recommendations for the future.

Conclusion

I believe that we can use conferences to help students write multiple-source papers. Conferencing provides an opportunity to respond individually to our students' papers with comments that both support and challenge their intellectual orientations toward divergent points of view. Although we need to keep in mind the limitations of developmental models such as Perry's, these schemes contribute strongly to the sociocognitive value of the writing conference.

Works Cited

Belenky, Mary Field, Blythe McVicker Clinchy, Nancy Rule-Goldberger, and Jill Mattuck Tarule. 1986. *Women's Ways of Knowing: The Development of Self, Voice, and Mind.* New York: Basic Books.

Bizzell, Patricia. 1984. "William Perry and Liberal Education." *College English* 5 (September): 447–54.

Clinchy, Blythe, and Claire Zimmerman. 1982. "Epistemology and Agency in the Development of Undergraduate Women." In *The Undergraduate Woman,* ed. Pamela J. Perun, 161–81. Lexington, Mass.: D. C. Heath.

Hays, Janice N. 1983. "The Development of Discursive Maturity in College Writers." In *The Writer's Mind: Writing as a Mode of Thinking,* ed. Janice N. Hays, Phyllis A. Roth, Jon R. Ramsey, and Robert D. Foulke, 127–44. Urbana, Ill.: National Council of Teachers of English.

Perry, William G. 1970. *Forum of Intellectual and Ethical Development in the College Years: A Scheme.* New York: Holt, Rinehart and Winston.

Widick, Carole, and Deborah Simpson. 1978. "Developmental Concepts in College Instruction." In *Encouraging Development in College Students,* ed. Clyde A. Parker, 27–59. Minneapolis: University of Minnesota Press.

IV Students Emerge as Independent Writers

Introduction to Section IV

Mary King
University of Akron

We have seen in section two that teacher and student need to select appropriate roles for their interactions in conferences in order to develop responsibility and higher-order thinking in novice writers. The essays in section three demonstrate the teacher's expertise in two areas: the teacher explicitly recommends to the student expert strategies of reading and writing, and the teacher tacitly practices collaborating to construct knowledge as part of the activities of the conference, without explicitly identifying that knowledge. The essays here in section four propose the following principle of writing pedagogy: students achieve independence in writing as an outgrowth of appropriate social interaction with experts, as described in section two, and appropriate use of expert strategies, as described in section three.

Inappropriate interactions or inappropriate strategies are likely to create dependence on the teacher and thus block the growth of higher-order thinking skills. An example of a strategy inappropriate for fostering independence (though it has value for other purposes) is direct instruction, the practice that most readily comes to mind when the word *teaching* is mentioned. The following description of direct instruction vividly shows the problem:

> In direct instruction, the teacher, in a face-to-face, reasonably formal manner, tells, shows, models, demonstrates, *teaches* the skill to be learned. The key word here is *teacher,* for it is the teacher who is in command of the learning situation and leads the lesson, as opposed to having instruction "directed" by a worksheet, kit, learning center, or workbook. (Baumann 1983, 287)

The student appears nowhere in this paradigm, which negates the novice-expert relationship that we have been describing: one of the most necessary strategies of the expert teacher is the art of fading into the background, progressively giving over responsibility as the student gains authority and control over the processes of writing.

The essays in this final section show that student writers can function with increasing success beyond the influence—indeed, beyond the ken—of their teachers in the classroom and in the writing center. The independent growth of writing skills is therefore mysterious, though not entirely so. Clearly, the activities of the classroom and the conversations in conference can combine to make that independent growth possible. In the cases reported here, the work in the writing conference involved clarifying and elaborating meaning so that the writer's increasing control of correct forms came as a side effect, not as the result of direct instruction in correct forms. As Janet Emig puts the matter, "Writing is predominantly learned rather than taught" (1983, 26). We might hypothesize that increased control in writing comes along with engagement in higher-order thinking, in keeping with cognitive theories about the human capacity for meaning making.

Cornelius Cosgrove, in "Conferencing for the 'Learning-Disabled': How We Might Really Help," points out that direct instruction in correct forms is unproductive even for those writers who have the greatest difficulty with correctness, those who have been labeled as "learning-disabled"; that the label is itself disabling; and that the atomistic pedagogies so often visited upon such students should be put aside in favor of more holistic, meaning-centered approaches. Direct instruction in correctness violates the first canon of instruction in higher-level thinking skills, self-regulation, and brings the discourse down to the lowest possible level. When writers focus narrowly on correctness, they can experience no aspiration to meaning making. Instead, they must submit to external authority. Cosgrove proposes to situate learning-disabled students in a setting where they can achieve independence in the same way that other students do—by writing, rewriting, and talking over their work with peers or with an expert in writing conferences.

Similarly, in "Fostering Spontaneous Dialect Shift in the Writing of African-American Students," Susanna Horn points out that such a dialect shift results from a teacher's knowing what to attend to and what to ignore in various stages of student writing. Horn shows the development of wide-ranging competence in successive drafts of several basic writing papers in which content alone was discussed with the writers. As they elaborated the content of their papers and made their meaning increasingly clear, these writers spontaneously shifted to standard verb forms. Conversely, when a conference for an English composition class focused attention on standard forms, the writer did not spontaneously elaborate and clarify meaning and in fact never attended sufficiently to constructing meaning. It seems reasonable to conclude that attention to a writer's higher-order concerns deepens attention to the entire range of concerns, whereas attention to lower-order concerns remains narrowly focused and superficial.

Paula Oye, in "Writing Problems beyond the Classroom: The Confidence Problem," reports on a student writer, referred to as Diane, whose independence grew as her confidence grew; Diane's writing also changed in ways only indirectly related to the activities of her writing conferences. Much of Oye's work consisted of supporting Diane's exploration of ideas and the connections among those ideas. Oye had to learn when to withdraw so that Diane could experience the excitement of her own success at constructing meaning and could gain confidence from the experience.

The question of why independence in writing may develop in unknown ways recalls Lauren Resnick's description of higher-order thinking. Several features of higher-order thinking are clearly related to independence in writing, but basic to all these is self-regulation. Resnick states: "We do not recognize higher order thinking in an individual when someone else 'calls the plays' at every step." Self-regulation, working outside of another's control or influence, is an invisible process. We can see only its results, though Resnick (1987, 3) identifies three related features that have special relevance to writing and that are discussed in the following paragraphs.

Higher-order thinking often yields multiple solutions, each with costs and benefits, rather than unique solutions. Writers may consult with a teacher, tutor, or peer about the merits of some of the solutions—or they may decide on their own, according to their own intentions for the piece. Thus, Horn observes that Rita chose to represent her children as speakers of Standard English in her final draft even though correctness had never been discussed by teacher, tutor, or peers during conferences.

Higher-order thinking is nonalgorithmic; that is, the path of action is not fully specified in advance. Writers work out the path in the process of writing. A corollary to this is that *only* the writers can determine the path. Oye worked out a path of action for her student's first paper, which Diane followed with some success, but when she was unable to repeat the process on a second paper, Oye realized that Diane had not really done it the first time— Oye had been the one engaging in higher-order thinking. Horn, too, points to a situation where a tutor worked out a path of action (looking only at verb forms for standard dialect features) and, in doing so, deflected Shawanda from the writer's work of elaborating meaning. Self-regulation is necessary for higher-order thinking.

Higher-order thinking is the hallmark of successful learning at all lev-els—not only the more advanced. Resnick points out that basic and higher-order skills cannot be clearly separated. For example, if we consider correct-ness in writing to be a basic skill, it *appears* that correctness could be sepa-rated out from the flow of students' written discourse and dealt with as a separate issue. But Horn shows with the example of Shawanda that to do so may cripple the writer's ability to employ the higher-order thinking skills used in constructing meaning. Cosgrove, too, suggests that engaging in higher-order thinking is crucial for the development of control in writing, even in situations where the most dramatic feature of a writer's work is the errors which riddle the page. These studies suggest that separating basic from higher-order skills is an inappropriate strategy for helping students achieve growth in writing.

Several of the essays in this book have shown students succeeding when they control the activities of the writing conference. Cosgrove urges that this control also be granted to students labeled as "learning-disabled." Oye and Horn demonstrate the successes that writers can enjoy in areas not dealt with in class or conference, when students emerge as independent writers. The move away from direct instruction, which teachers may at first have to practice as an act of faith, is here shown to be an absolute necessity. To persevere in practices based on the social construction of knowledge is to respect student capacity and to respect the primacy of meaning.

Works Cited

Baumann, J. F. 1983. "A Generic Comprehension Instructional Strategy." *Read-ing World* 22:284–94.

Emig, Janet. 1983. *The Web of Meaning: Essays on Writing, Teaching, Learning, and Thinking,* ed. Dixie Goswami and Maureen Butler. Upper Montclair, N.J.: Boynton/Cook.

Resnick, Lauren B. 1987. *Education and Learning to Think.* Washington, D.C.: National Academy Press.

9 Conferencing for the "Learning-Disabled": How We Might Really Help

Cornelius Cosgrove
Slippery Rock University

I have become puzzled by the label *learning-disabled*. Shifting definitions frustrate attempts to understand the condition, and proliferating sets of criteria frustrate attempts to identify and diagnose its sufferers. Clear distinctions between "learning-disabled" and "normal" students have not been established; in the area of writing, differences are of degree rather than kind. And there remains, stubbornly, the reality faced by teachers and students—some people have inordinate difficulty reading and writing accurately. The fact is, however, that the strategies recommended by professionals for teaching composition to students with learning disabilities are strategies that most of us would use with any writer who was having difficulty: whole language, writing process approaches, and conferencing. These strategies demonstrate the methods that experts use for approaching writing problems. They are appropriate because they circumvent the writer's difficulties by emphasizing meaning over form. And they offer flexible instruction that can be adapted to the student's needs. Some history of the field and a brief survey of the literature may clarify the appropriateness of writing conference practices for this population.

The learning disabilities field is based on a medical explanation for a curious phenomenon—the existence of children of easily observable intelligence who are failing in their formal schooling. It is a field fraught with terms like *dyslexia*, *dysgraphia*, *aphasia*, and *neurological dysfunction*. It is not just a set of theories but an elaborate taxonomy that has grown up around those theories. The field is occupied by a set of experts who have either developed or thoroughly learned those theories and classifications. Confronted

---

An earlier version of this essay appeared in the conference proceedings of the East Central Writing Centers Association for 1989.

95

by yet another bastion of specialized knowledge, the generalists who usually teach writing courses and staff writing centers naturally tend to leave
the students labeled as learning-disabled to those specifically trained to help
them.

Nevertheless, wanting to learn how to serve such students, I have made
sustained forays into the field's professional literature. I have examined texts
used to introduce special education majors to learning disabilities theory. I
have more than sampled the pages of several journals in the field of special
education. I have read some of the most trenchant critics of learning disabilities theory, critics who are found both within special education and outside it, particularly among sociologists. I have reviewed the literature of composition specialists that addresses the problem of learning-disabled students
or that discusses issues directly related to the teaching of such students.

On the basis of extensive research into learning disabilities theory as
viewed by the fields of special education, sociology, and composition, I have
reached a few conclusions which may have significance for writing instructors who work with students labeled as learning-disabled. Perhaps the most
disconcerting result of my investigation is that I am now inclined to treat the
identification of a student writer as learning-disabled with some skepticism.
For after a quarter-century of intense growth and even more intense debate,
the learning disabilities field has failed to define the condition satisfactorily,
or to explain its causes, or to develop a diagnostic approach that can clearly
identify those who have a learning disability and those who do not. This is
not an occasion to explore in detail all the theoretical problems which have
beset researchers in the discipline. Suffice it to say that when the learning
disabilities field really "took off" in the early to mid 1960s, the condition
was usually defined in terms of its presumed cause—an unobtrusive neurological impairment that prevented obviously intelligent children from per-
forming adequately in school. Unfortunately, even when such extraordinary
diagnostic measures as neurological examinations and electroencephalograms
were employed, it proved very difficult to determine that any brain damage
or dysfunction was present in the subject, or that any dysfunction which did
exist could explain the subject's academic difficulties (Coles 1978, 322–
26). Consequently, as the field grew, the focus of the definitions shifted from
causes to symptoms and, in particular, to the supposed gap between a child's
tested intelligence and academic performance. As might have been expected,
debate has raged ever since concerning how great that gap has to be before
someone is labeled as learning-disabled, and what formulas ought to be used
in determining whether a gap even exists.

During the 1970s and early 1980s, the number of definitions of the term *learning disability* grew; as did the number of methods for determining whether a child should be so labeled; as did, understandably, the number of children who were so labeled. Evidence appeared that significant numbers of children had been and were being misidentified as learning-disabled. One sampling of eight hundred Colorado learning-disabled students found that less than half "had characteristics that are associated in federal law and professional literature with the definitions of learning disabilities" (Shepard, Smith, and Vojir 1983, 328). A study of 248 third, fifth, and twelfth graders who were *not* considered learning-disabled demonstrated that a considerable percentage could have been so labeled using most of the seventeen different sets of criteria that the researchers found in the professional literature. Using one particular "statistical discrepancy" formula, 84 percent of the "normal" twelfth graders *could* have been identified as learning-disabled (Ysseldyke, Algozzine, and Epps 1983, 162–63). The same researchers looked at fifty fourth graders in two metropolitan school districts who had already been identified as learning-disabled and discovered two students who did not qualify using any of the seventeen sets of criteria (165).

Some critics of the learning disabilities field have argued that the category has been used to "mask" environmental causes for poor academic performance, such as inadequate teaching, curricula, and school facilities, or adverse social conditions (Carrier 1983, 948). During the 1970s an eight-year study of school districts in the Southwest concluded that "the percentage of Blacks being placed into special education . . . has steadily increased from a point that was already disproportionately high in the beginning," and directly attributed that increase to the creation of the learning-disabled category (Tucker 1980, 99).

In consideration of all the difficulties described above, certain special education professionals have concluded that the focus of research ought to be shifted away from the broad category of *learning-disabled* and toward its "subtypes" (Keller and Hallahan 1987, 18) or "subsets," such as aphasia or "accurately defined dyslexia" (Cruickshank, Morse, and Johns 1980, 6). In the meantime, what are postsecondary teachers and writing center staff supposed to do with what could be described as a pedagogical and administrative nightmare? How do we react to a student who is identified as learning-disabled? What is a learning disability? If we can figure that one out, then how can we be sure that this particular student is disabled? If we determine that, then how can we know which instructional approach would be most appropriate?

A possible course would be to treat all students as if neither the label nor the condition itself exists, since no satisfactory definition of the term *learning disabilities* has been developed. There are historical and logical arguments to support this position. As Mike Rose ably points out, to accept the medically influenced terminology of the learning disabilities field is to run the historically verifiable risk of also accepting a behaviorist approach to writing that is "atomistic . . . error-centered, and linguistically reductive" (1985, 343). Accept the medical paradigm, and writing becomes merely a set of skills that can be "diagnosed" and "remediated" through the kinds of decontextualized "therapies" found in workbooks and other vehicles of programmed instruction. Out the window goes the process-oriented whole language approach that for many of us has been the main justification for the resurgence of writing centers and writing instruction in general over the past two decades.

Therefore, the unquestioning acceptance of medical explanations for difficulties in learning and using written language could threaten the empowerment of both writing teachers and writing centers. That might be an acceptable turn of events if those same explanations served to empower the students themselves. Unfortunately, both logic and human nature seem to argue against that possibility. One director of reading and writing programs at a Michigan two-year college has warned "that the 'disease' model of interpreting student language and learning problems" could result in "exclusionary practices" and "unwarranted anxiety and fears" on the part of affected students (Franke 1986, 171). Simple logic suggests that it would be perfectly understandable for a student to receive the news that he or she has a learning disability with feelings of helplessness and resignation. After all, if one's situation is biologically determined, then how can remedial instruction improve or eliminate it (Christensen, Gerber, and Everhart 1986, 330)? And how can you tell students that their poor intellectual performance is caused by neurological impairment *and* that they are functioning below their potential? Would not the students' potential be determined, at least in part, by their impairments (322)?

These logical flaws, however, will not allow us simply to dismiss the whole theoretical structure of learning disabilities and to carry on as if they either did not exist or did not matter. Such an attitude would be both ingenuous and impractical. At this point, a multitude of school children in this country have already been labeled as learning-disabled, and many have defined themselves in terms of this disability. Of equal importance is the observation that the problems that many of these students have with written language are real enough, even if the reasons for their existence are unknown and the names that they have been given are logically and empirically inadequate.

We are left, therefore, with a second option—to admit the existence of both the category and students who define themselves academically as members of the category. It should be understood, however, that this admission does not necessarily require us to alter our pedagogical approach radically when assisting learning-disabled students. Indeed, some recent experiences and research findings within special education argue for staying with what we now believe is the most effective form of writing instruction—one-to-one peer and professional tutoring that guides students through the process of generating written language. Though these methods are most readily found in writing centers, they can be used by classroom teachers.

During the past decade, many special education practitioners have turned to group learning, role-playing, and peer tutoring as appropriate techniques for teaching learning-disabled students reading and writing (Keller and Hallahan 1987, 22–24). A 1986 review of research into the effectiveness of peer tutoring concluded that students who have been categorized as learning-disabled, behaviorally disordered, or mentally retarded "experience academic and social benefits by functioning as either a tutor or tutee" (Osguthorpe and Scruggs 1986, 22). It must be added that almost all of the twenty-six examined studies dealt with statistically measurable growth in reading, spelling, or mathematics.

Other effective strategies for teaching composition skills to students labeled as learning-disabled are oral activities, conferencing, and practice in writing whole discourse. Janet Lerner's special education text on learning disabilities, which has been through several editions, contains a developmental sequence for teaching "written expression" in which she recommends much interaction between pupil and teacher while employing the techniques of dictation, copying, and rewriting (1981, 350–51). She concludes with this admonition: "Give the child many experiences in writing" (351). Eva Weiner has argued that oral reading of student writing by both the teacher and the writer during conferences is the best way to overcome syntactic and grammatical difficulties and to develop self-editing ability. "Formal grammar lessons," she writes, "are less effective than the process of editing personal writing in making the abstractions of grammar rules meaningful" (1980, 52).

Through the examination of a case study, J. R. Moulton and M. S. Bader, two Massachusetts public school teachers, illustrate how having "language-disabled" students develop a piece of writing through "manageable stages," with peer or student-teacher conferences conducted at each stage, can improve "their ability to explore their ideas and enhance their written expression" (1985, 161). Prewriting began with a model, then freewritten notes, and then the telling of the student's story to a classmate, who asked questions and made suggestions. By conferencing, the teacher guided the student through the stages of drafting, revising, and proofreading (163-69). Another study, this one conducted in Arizona by Candace Bos, has examined the writing of "mildly handicapped" intermediate school students whose teachers were using a process-oriented approach. Bos describes "increases . . . in the length and structural complexity of the written pieces, the amount and quality of planning, and students' perceptions concerning their competence as writers." Moreover, improvement is reported in "thematic maturity, vocabulary, and overall coherence and organization" (1985, 522-23).

The reason for this brief literature review, of course, is to demonstrate that conferencing and process orientation are what some teachers of the learning-disabled are concluding their students ought to have when learning composition. When we couple this observation with the realization that clear distinctions between "learning-disabled" and "normal" students have not been established, we must conclude that when working with learning-disabled students, writing instructors who make use of conferencing should not change their pedagogical approach in any significant way. If a writing instructor is convinced that formal grammar drill and mastery learning approaches are not the most appropriate way to help developing writers, then it would be a mistake for that same professional to assume that those methods are somehow more appropriate when assisting writers identified as learning-disabled.

When the learning disabilities literature describes how the writing of learning-disabled students differs from that of "normal" students, it commonly uses terms of degree rather than kind. Phrases like "more than" and "greater difficulty with" and "less apt to" occur with some frequency; moreover, any composition or writing specialist will be struck by the familiarity of the difficulties often directly attributed to the learning disabled. Take, for example, these two quotations from Moulton and Bader:

> language-disabled students . . . do not spontaneously develop strategies for writing, and, consequently, their written production does not realize their true potential for expression. (161)

> After years of trying to write under heavy constraints, many language-disabled students in secondary school hurry through a writing assignment and produce the safest, shortest composition they can. (166)

Drop the phrase "language-disabled," and those utterances could have been made by any writing specialist discussing any student.

Consequently, a message should be published among special education teachers and students that conferencing and process-oriented writing instruction offer what writers need, regardless of evaluative distinctions. Writing centers can also develop programs that would give students labeled as learning-disabled an opportunity to become peer tutors for other writers. Research indicates that, with training, learning-disabled students who tutor demonstrate significant improvements in both academic performance and attitude (Osguthorpe and Scruggs 1986, 21).

To conclude, writing instruction can best help students by focusing on discourse rather than on error. An informed approach to the development of writers recognizes that writing individualizes writers and proclaims their uniqueness. It is the writing itself which empowers the students. And it is the knowledge of what writing does that empowers effective writing instruction. By listening and guiding, rather than drilling and categorizing, skilled writing instructors can best help those students who have been labeled as learning-disabled.

Works Cited

Bos, Candace S. 1988. "Process-Oriented Writing: Instructional Implications for Mildly Handicapped Students." *Exceptional Children* 54 (6): 521–27.

Carrier, James G. 1983. "Masking the Social in Educational Knowledge: The Case of Learning Disability Theory." *American Journal of Sociology* 88:948–74.

Christensen, Carol A., Michael M. Gerber, and Robert B. Everhart. 1986. "Toward a Sociological Perspective on Learning Disabilities." *Educational Theory* 36:317–31.

Coles, Gerald S. 1978. "The Learning-Disabilities Test Battery: Empirical and Social Issues." *Harvard Educational Review* 48:313–40.

Cruickshank, William M., William C. Morse, and Jeannie Johns. 1980. *Learning Disabilities: The Struggle from Adolescence to Adulthood.* Syracuse, N.Y.: Syracuse University Press.

Franke, Thomas L. 1986. "Dyslexia and the College English Teacher." *Teaching English in the Two-Year College* 13:171–77.

Keller, Clayton E., and Daniel P. Hallahan. 1987. *Learning Disabilities: Issues and Instructional Interventions.* Washington, D.C.: National Education Association.

Lerner, Janet W. 1981. *Learning Disabilities: Theories, Diagnosis, and Teaching Strategies.* 3d ed. Boston: Houghton Mifflin.

Moulton, J. R., and M. S. Bader. 1985. "The Writing Process: A Powerful Approach for the Language-Disabled Student." *Annals of Dyslexia* 35:161-73.

Osguthorpe, Russell T., and Thomas E. Scruggs. 1986. "Special Education Students as Tutors: A Review and Analysis." *Remedial and Special Education* 7 (4): 15-26.

Rose, Mike. 1985. "The Language of Exclusion: Writing Instruction at the University." *College English* 47:341-59.

Shepard, Lorrie A., Mary Lee Smith, and Carol P. Vojir. 1983. "Characteristics of Pupils Identified as Learning Disabled." *American Educational Research Journal* 20:309-31.

Tucker, James A. 1980. "Ethnic Proportions in Classes for the Learning Disabled: Issues in Nonbiased Assessment." *Journal of Special Education* 14:93-105.

Weiner, Eva S. 1980. "Diagnostic Evaluation of Writing Skills." *Journal of Learning Disabilities* 13:48-53.

Ysseldyke, James, Bob Algozzine, and Susan Epps. 1983. "A Logical and Empirical Analysis of Current Practice in Classifying Students as Handicapped." *Exceptional Children* 50:160-66.

10 Fostering Spontaneous Dialect Shift in the Writing of African-American Students

Susanna Horn
University of Akron

Even the most experienced among us sometimes forget that the purpose of a writing conference is to support students in their endeavors to express their ideas clearly in writing. It is not our duty merely to aid them in producing "correct" papers for particular writing assignments, nor is such a reductionist approach in the students' best interest. Our first and foremost aim is to help students concentrate on the content of their writing so that they are better able to write a piece that has significant meaning for themselves and for their readers. After that, we help students develop and demonstrate their linguistic competence in a way that will aid them in their efforts to become part of the academic community. For speakers of an African-American dialect, demonstrating linguistic competence in academic settings can mean taking extra time during editing to make a conscious switch from the spoken dialect to the written code. Tutors must remember that such competence already exists in many university students and that waiting until the editing stage before commenting on dialect concerns is imperative; once the student is sure about content, many dialect-associated errors are spontaneously eliminated from subsequent drafts. Even for those students who cannot easily shift to the written code, the editing that the switch requires must remain one of the last items of consideration. Insisting that editing be kept the final step in composing maintains "students' right to their own language," as urged by the Conference on College Composition and Communication (Committee on CCCC Language Statement 1974), and reinforces the importance of teaching the language of wider communication, as Geneva Smitherman-Donaldson has recently reminded us (1987).

An earlier version of this essay appeared in the conference proceedings of the East Central Writing Centers Association for 1987.

Unfortunately, the time frame of a student's writing process does not necessarily conform to the timetable of a college course, and it is not always possible for a writer to proceed beyond the content stage and through editing and proofreading in time to meet a teacher's deadline. When timetables do not mesh, students turn in papers that may be flawed in any number of ways, especially in matters of correctness of grammar, spelling, or syntax. This problem is most frustrating when a student who has diligently concentrated on making meaning is confronted with an instructor who is particularly reactive to performance errors, especially those errors that are typically associated with speakers of an African-American dialect. Such a situation may lead both instructors and students to focus on matters of correctness too soon in the writing process, often to the point of ignoring the larger matters of organization and development. Therefore, as professional writing center tutors, we must remind ourselves and our students that good writing requires plenty of time; a premature emphasis on the product will shut down students' creative, analytical, or expository thinking. By refusing to acquiesce to the student's ever-present desire for closure, we can help maintain the writer's mental momentum, and thus provide sufficient time—time to think, time to write, time to revise, time to edit, and perhaps time to begin again.

I am still amazed at just how competent in writing all native speakers of English can become when they have sufficient time and when they are first given help in the areas of content and development rather than in grammar, syntax, and spelling, as important as those areas may be. The extent of this competence became strikingly clear when I did a small linguistic study of dialect shift between drafts written by African-American students taking a basic writing class at the University of Akron. Since many students have trouble meeting the numerous demands of the written code, my initial aim was to count and describe the multitude of errors that I expected to find in their final drafts. Predictably, I found a number of distracting errors, such as missing or incorrect noun and verb endings, but to find enough errors to develop a meaningful study, I had to dig into the rough drafts and freewritings. There such errors abounded. Now my question was, how did these students correct their errors on their final drafts? Given the tendency of our process-oriented basic writing teachers to ignore errors so early in the term, and given the collaborative nature of our basic writing program, I felt that I could only attribute such a notable decline in errors to spontaneous, collaborative learning and/or to individual language competency, rather than to the teachers' intervention or insistence upon correctness.

My findings reinforced my intuition that the students whom we see in our midwestern university writing center are intelligent adults who are quite conscious that the dialect of the classroom and of writing is fairly close to the dialect that they hear spoken on the evening news. These students are expert at switching styles when appropriate, for they will often say to a teacher a sentence such as, "My sister is very inconsiderate," and then promptly make an aside to a classmate such as, "She don't be doing no work; she alway be leavin' it for me." Such students are capable of correcting many of their own errors *if* such errors are ignored until the appropriate stage of writing, which is editing.

When they have time, in fact, students often correct their own writing in remarkable ways. The following examples of spontaneous dialect shift show what typical basic writers can do. These students worked on content in collaboration groups in class, or with a tutor in the writing center; they were not specifically pushed to correct their grammar. Though the papers are far from perfect, there are significant increases in correct verb forms. Bear in mind that the changes shown here were student initiated; teachers were not insisting upon correctness at this early point in the semester.

Tony's focused freewriting about his fight with a friend was less than a page long, disappointingly short. By the time he wrote his final draft, however, he had good control of his sentences and verb forms. In his focused freewriting Tony wrote:

> I saw red and just clocked-out and commence to beating, beating up my teammate who was my friend. After the fight a funny thing happen, we both apologized and went on as if nothing had happen.

The rough draft was more elaborated and somewhat corrected:

> I saw red and just clocked-out and commence to beating up my close friend who was also a teammate. Usually if two friends fought like we did they no longer would be friends. After our fight a funny thing happened we both apologized and went on as if nothing had ever happened.

The final draft was 50 percent longer than the rough draft and showed Tony's awareness of the greater demands required in a "public" copy of his work, including proper endings on newly added verbs:

> I saw red and just clocked-out and commenced to beating up my close friend, who was also a teammate of mine. Some girls on the girls track team started yelling for the other boys and the coach to

break up the fight. Dunn, another friend and teammate of ours, was just standing there watching in shock, as we threw and punched each other around like animals. After the fight I was confused about it. I knew I really started the fight, but why? Sam was confused as to how the fight started also. Usually if two friends fought like we did they would no longer be friends. After our fight a unusual thing happened. We both apologized to each other and went on as if nothing had ever happened.

Through a process of collaboration and rewriting, Tony's paper grew from two sentences with five *-ed* verbs (three lacking endings) to nine sentences with eleven *-ed* verbs, all complete with endings. He did not have a textbook with verb tense exercises; he did not have a checklist of features to edit; and he did not receive directions from a teacher or tutor to reread for correct verb forms. The exclusive focus of attention by all readers and collaborators was on telling the story, elaborating meaning. Somehow during the process, Tony recognized his need to switch to the written code, and he produced prose of almost perfect correctness, without a single verb form error.

Successive drafts by another student show clearly that her struggle was with her dialect rather than with her knowledge of verb forms. Rita wrote about how the good manners of the children of some friends have influenced her children to improve their manners. She revised her own rough draft so thoroughly that in places it was difficult to follow, amid all the numbers, scratched out lines, and additions. For better or for worse, her changes clearly reveal what she deemed appropriate in a final draft for a college course. In her rough draft Rita quotes her children:

"Mom, those kids alway *[crossed out]* just be trying to fake you out. They're are not that nice."

The final draft reads:

"Mom, those kids are trying to fake you out, they're not that nice."

Later in the rough draft Rita writes:

"Oh that why they come to spend the nite with us all the time, you be trying to give us one of those sub bliminal messages . . ."

In the final draft Rita has her children say:

"That's why they spend the night with us all the time. You must be
trying to give us one of those sub-liminal messages . . ."

Either Rita did not understand that quotations need not be grammatical, or
she simply could not bear to have her children use anything other than Standard English in her paper for a university course. Whatever the case, Rita's
choice to shift the dialect of her children's comments demonstrates that she,
like many bidialectal students, is quite capable of making conscious choices
about her writing style. Neither Tony nor Rita needed a professional editor.
They just needed to be given the time to incorporate their existing knowledge of the written code into their writing.

Unfortunately, there is another side to the story. We often see students
whose own concern with correctness has seemingly blocked their ability to
write meaningfully. Sometimes even well-intentioned instructors can inadvertently cause a student to pay attention to verb forms too soon. For example, Shawanda was taking the writing-about-literature semester of English composition. Her instructor had commented on the content of four
successive drafts, and Shawanda dutifully changed and/or improved each
one. However, she either forgot or simply did not take the time to edit her
paper and received a grade of D on the final version because of incorrect
regular past-tense and third-person-singular present-tense verbs. Later, in
the Writing Center, a tutor patiently went through the paper with the desper-
ate student, sentence by sentence, and reassured her that she did indeed know
English and merely had to catch her errors before turning in a final paper—
so far, so good.

However, as Shawanda was writing her next paper, she misinterpreted
the tutor's encouragement. Because of her failure in her first paper, Shawanda
was eager to demonstrate her competence in the written code and became
unwilling to postpone editing her work until after she had established her
meaning. On Shawanda's next paper the -s and -ed endings were all properly included; however, meaning had fallen victim to correctness. Simply
put, her sentences often did not make sense in regard to the play that she was
discussing, so she needed to go back to "say what you mean; worry about
correctness later." Shawanda began again.

Interestingly, although this disappointing paper had all the -ed and -s endings written in the right places, Shawanda dropped every one of them as she
concentrated on content while reading the paper aloud to me, thus reinforc-

ing the long-held sociolinguistic contention that, for a speaker, meaning resides in the native dialect. I am particularly encouraged when students use their native dialect as they explain to me what they want to say on paper; it not only shows me that they trust me not to censor their speech, but, more importantly, it indicates that they are actively making meaning for themselves. As teachers and tutors, we must not gag the natural, outer manifestation of the students' "inner speech" before they have a chance to figure out what they want to say. We can always work on the fine points of Standard English later, after meaning has been established, even if the student must ask the teacher for a deadline extension to do so.

When the time to edit does arrive, both bidialectal students and those who cannot yet easily switch to the standard form benefit far more from learning an editing process than from getting their papers "corrected" in the Writing Center. Teaching students how to find and correct their own errors by having them read aloud again and again and again takes a few concentrated sessions, but affords students an invaluable way of looking at their own work. For example, when reading his or her paper aloud to a tutor, a student will often add standard word endings which do not appear in the manuscript. When such a student is ready to attend to error, it is the tutor's job to remind the student that he or she is speaking the correct forms, but that these forms do not appear on the paper. It is then helpful for the tutor to require the student to read aloud again, pointing out the specific omissions or additions only when the student cannot readily do so. Those students who continue to omit endings both on paper and when reading aloud can be reassured that even the most educated among us often slur or drop endings when speaking and that all speakers of English must remember to add -s or -ed to our nouns and verbs when we write, no matter what we actually voice in conversation. Almost paradoxically, the tutor helps students train their ears to hear the very endings that are so often dropped in speech. This approach draws upon students' awareness of mass-media speech and familiarity with print, thus giving them a base from which to continue developing mastery of the written code. (For a detailed account of a well-known study using a similar technique, see David Bartholomae 1980.)

Closer to home, my colleague Gayle Irish did a training study with six students at the University of Akron and Kent State University. Her objective was "to discover a technique that would allow all students to correct at least 50% of their errors by drawing on the knowledge that they already possess" (1984, 227). After focusing on the higher-order concern of achieving clarity, students were spontaneously able to correct 24 percent of their errors while reading their papers aloud for the first time. After three sessions of training, some students were able to correct 60 to 80 percent of such errors. Thus the results of bringing students' own linguistic competence to their attention has nearly miraculous results for those students who are ready and willing. Fortunately, what at first appears to be a slow, time-consuming tutoring session may well be among the most time-efficient teaching that a tutor can do, for such an approach gives writers an all-important confidence in their ability to think and to manipulate their native language.

Whether our bidialectal students are dealing with still-incomplete papers or grappling with editing concerns, patience is imperative. We must first allow students the time to discover what it is they want to say and then encourage them to express their ideas, free from the constraints of "correct English." The Task Force on Curriculum Design and Construction of the Center for Black Studies reminds us that "standard English should be viewed as a tool to aid in the attainment of particular goals and that both standard English and Black English can be part of one's language system" (Simkins 1981, 320). If the tutor is respectfully slow to make corrections, students can maintain their own social dialect and still learn the written code of the academy. If not pressured too soon, students may edit their work even more spontaneously than any of us have imagined.

Writing Center staff members are as bewildered as Geneva Smitherman-Donaldson regarding how students actually learn the complex skill of code switching (Smitherman-Donaldson and Van Dijk 1988, 169), but if we are alert to the needs and talents of each writer, we may find that we often can open our minds, close our handbooks, and have faith in the intelligence and linguistic competence of the students whom we encourage. Our job is to allow students to become better writers, not merely to produce better writing.

Works Cited

Bartholomae, David. 1980. "The Study of Error." *College Composition and Communication* 31 (October): 253–69.

Committee on CCCC Language Statement. 1974. "Students' Right to Their Own Language." *College Composition and Communication* 25 (Fall): 1–32.

Irish, Gayle. 1984. "So Let Them Perform: How to Deal with the Performance-Based Error of Basic Writers." *Teaching English in the Two-Year College* 10 (Spring): 227–33.

Simkins, Gary. 1981. "Curriculum Design and Construction." In *Black English and the Education of Black Children and Youth: Proceedings of the National Invitational Symposium on the* King *Decision,* ed. Geneva Smitherman, 320–22. Detroit: Wayne State University Press.

Smitherman-Donaldson, Geneva. 1987. "Toward a National Policy on Language." *College English* 40 (January): 29–36.

Smitherman-Donaldson, Geneva, and Teun A. Van Dijk. 1988. *Discourse and Discrimination.* Detroit: Wayne State University Press.

11 Writing Problems beyond the Classroom: The Confidence Problem

Paula M. Oye
Michigan Technological University

It is often easy for the composition teacher to spot the very good and the very poor students in a class. Good students write articulate, polished papers and lead class discussions with perceptive, pithy comments. Poor students may barely be able to write coherent sentences, much less readable papers, and have difficulty answering even direct questions. The instructor can encourage prize pupils and earmark those who are in obvious trouble for individual help with basic writing skills, but there is a large group of students whose problems often go unattended in the classroom and who, consequently, never have the opportunity to realize their potential as writers.

These B-minus or C-level students spend the term on the edge of the instructor's perception, writing competent but dull or superficial papers in an undistinguished style, giving only adequate answers to direct questions, and rarely contributing voluntarily to class discussion. They may give the impression of being indifferent, lazy, or even mildly hostile to being asked to study English, or they may simply seem shy and overwhelmed in the classroom. But they are not failing; they will get by. Even if the teacher should notice that some of these wallflower students have the potential to blossom into really good writers, there is little time or opportunity for the classroom instructor to give them the prolonged and concentrated individual attention that they need to overcome their reticence and develop their writing skills. As David Taylor mentions in chapter 2, content skills and attitude are inextricably bound. My writing center colleagues and I have found that the writing conference provides the informal atmosphere, personal attention, and opportunity to form working relationships based on trust, which these students need in order to develop a confidence reflected both in their

---

An earlier version of this essay appeared in the conference proceedings of the East Central Writing Centers Association for 1983.

writing and in their classroom participation. They need this confidence to cope with the uncertainty, the increased effort, and the need for self-regulation that characterize the higher-level thinking skills that they must utilize in college-level writing courses. The following case study is an example of the Cinderella-like growth that students can achieve. Not all people make such dramatic progress, but most show the same pattern of improvement as a result of their one-to-one work with experienced tutors.

An eighteen-year-old first-year chemical engineering student, whom I will call Diane, was assigned to me during the fourth week of the ten-week fall quarter. Her composition instructor, who had referred her to the Writing Lab, told me that Diane needed help in focusing and developing her papers, but that she seemed reticent and suspicious of the teacher's suggestions. As Taylor points out, trust and empathy can play key roles in intellectual development. Diane's instructor felt that she might be more receptive to assistance from someone who was not such an obvious authority figure.

Diane shuffled into the lab for her appointment, wearing jeans and a letter jacket from a local high school. Her responses were polite but barely audible as she gave me her address and phone number for her student file. She did not volunteer any information, and my attempts at conversation were met with courteous but brief responses. When I asked her what she thought were her biggest problems with writing, she pushed a partly written paper over to me, shrugged, and, without looking up, said, "I don't know. I never did very good in English. It's hard to think of enough to write about. I guess I just can't write." The paper in front of me, a half-finished description of her high school cross-country coach, showed that Diane's low opinion of her ability was an exaggeration. The following excerpt of the first draft illustrates the tone and style of the piece:

> The one person who has made the strongest impression on me is my high school cross country coach. Mr. Arne Henderson. He was a tall man with long legs. He was built like a runner. At first glance he looked kind of intimidating, but this wasn't true.
>
> You could tell he loved to coach. He was concerned about anything that bothered you. If you ever had complaint about a teammate or a workout he wanted to hear about it, and if you had a problem outside of running, his door was always open if you wanted to talk.

Grammar, mechanics, and syntax, while not perfect, were passable, but the paper lacked detail and a strong voice. She had written a tight, sterile description: the coach was a two-dimensional figure who needed to be fleshed out by accounts of her experiences with him, character-revealing details, and a dominant impression. Diane needed to put herself into the paper.

This plain, objective style is often found in the writing of the engineering and technology students who come to the writing center. Since most of them read very little except their textbooks, they are exposed primarily to a direct, factual writing style. In addition, many of these students see no point in "flowery" writing, an attitude that has led them into confrontations with English teachers throughout high school. Diane was no exception, and it seemed that her personality only reinforced these no-nonsense views. Her clothing, short-cropped hair, straightforward and unadorned speech, and personal reserve indicated that she was as direct and practical as her writing. The problem was to get her to trust me enough to relate some of the personal details that would help her paper, but I felt that an attempt at instant camaraderie would only earn her contempt.

Coincidentally, Diane and I lived only a few blocks from each other, and my daughter had just started to attend Diane's old high school. I mentioned that my daughter might profit from some pointers on which teachers to avoid and what to expect from the track coach. Diane responded. I was no longer an alien—I was a real person who knew the neighborhood and had a child in her school. She began to tell me some of her experiences with her coach, and I suggested that she include them in her paper as support for her general statements. If she could tell me about her coach so well, I said, she could surely write down what she had said. Diane seemed skeptical, but we spent the rest of the session writing a list of details. Over the next two weeks and two more drafts, she was able to think of more and more detail to add, and a dominant impression developed, as the opening paragraphs of her final draft illustrate:

> There are many people in my life that have made strong impressions on me: my teachers, parents, and friends, but one person seems to stick out in my mind, my high school cross country coach, Mr. Arne Henderson.
>
> He was a tall man, with long muscular legs and a lean body. He was built like a runner. At first glance, he looked kind of intimidating, because he was so tall and he seemed like the sober type, but this wasn't true. He was slow to anger, and he was always quick to smile or offer a word of encouragement.

We had little time to work on style or mechanics, but the paper came back with a grade of B and a compliment from her instructor on the effective use of detail. When Diane saw that my suggestions had paid off and that she could actually produce what the teacher wanted, her confidence in herself and in me began, very slowly, to increase.

The next class assignment was to write a narrative of a personal experience. When Diane brought in her first draft, it seemed as if our efforts on the last paper had been useless. The writing was as terse and dry as the first draft of the first paper had been. Although she responded much more readily and easily to my attempts to elicit detail, she had not been able to add the relevant detail on her own. In addition, the story, an account of cutting a class and being seen by her teacher, lacked a purpose and climax, and suggestions from both her instructor and me that she change her topic failed to sway her. I had her tell me the story several times, hoping to find some of the missing narrative detail and suspense. How had she felt when she was discovered? What had her teacher said? How had he looked? But her recollections were vague, and if she had any emotional reaction, she was reluctant to reveal it.

Diane worked hard, revising the paper several times, but when the paper came back with a grade of C, she was dejected. I saw her confidence fading and feared that she would give up on the writing center. Moreover, I was troubled that she evidently had been unable to apply any of the techniques that I assumed she had learned from her first paper. She had merely accepted my suggestions without having learned the principles behind them. I felt that I had fallen into the same trap, mentioned by Mary King in chapter 7, to which literature instructors, among others, succumb: doing all the analysis, directing too much, and failing to teach anything at all.

When I saw Diane's name on my winter quarter schedule, I was relieved. She had not given up. Most composition teachers at our university devote the second quarter to the research paper. Diane was to choose for a research project an issue prominent in the decade following her birth and then write a series of three increasingly closely focused papers on the issue. Since the information gathering is the responsibility of the student, often a tutor can do little but offer encouragement and guidance during the early phases of the research. Would Diane be motivated enough to do a thorough job of research without any direction? Furthermore, the paper was to be more than a report; it was to be a personal interpretation of the issue. Now she would have to express and support an opinion. Would she be willing to take a personal stand? I wondered, before our first appointment, whether I would have to try to gain her trust all over again. But when she came in and pulled out the rough draft of her first assignment, she greeted me, if not like an old friend, at least as an acquaintance.

I read the following introduction to the paper:

> Nineteen sixty three was an exciting time to live. Women were becoming more daring and outgoing, children were defying the moral codes of their parents, and blacks were campaigning vigorously for their civil rights. To sum it up briefly, 1963 was a year filled with rebellion, it was a period of great social change and disorder.

Here was a new problem. Her thesis statement was broad enough to include all the information that she had gathered about the 1960s, but it was so vague that it could not be properly developed. She admitted that she had been uncertain of what she wanted to say. Besides, she said, as she pointed to a note from her instructor suggesting that she might focus on the women's movement for her major research topic, her real interest was the civil rights movement. I was surprised. Diane had known all along the topic on which she wanted to focus. It seemed her faith in herself was improving: she had committed herself to declaring an interest, and had been confident enough to let me know that she disagreed with the direction in which she felt her instructor was steering her. But she still lacked enough self-assurance to talk with her teacher. I acted as a go-between, a role often filled by tutors, explaining to the instructor that Diane wanted to focus on the civil rights movement, and explaining to Diane that her teacher's suggestion had not been an attempt to influence her choice of topic.

In the process of organizing her research papers, Diane and I talked far more than we had before. I could remember the civil rights marches and Martin Luther King, Jr. "Were the magazine articles true?" she wanted to know. "What did King sound like when he spoke? Did the police really use attack dogs?" Her interest and curiosity had shifted the balance of conversation between us: she was now talking more than I. Sarah Warshauer Freedman and Anne Marie Katz (1987) have noted that changes such as this in the conference dialogue indicate that students are becoming more assertive and using the conference to address their needs. In these exchanges, I learned about Diane's beliefs and principles. She, in turn, was uncovering so much new information in her research that she seemed to want to sift and organize it by talking to someone. We did very little writing during our sessions. Instead, Diane came in with stacks of notes, quoted passages, and sections of partially written drafts, and we tried to put together a clear picture of the causes and dynamics of the civil rights movement. She still needed a specific thesis for her paper, but I hoped that by helping her make connections among all the isolated pieces of information, I could encourage her to develop the thesis by herself. I did not want to repeat my mistake of being too directive.

Diane came in one day with a nearly completed draft of the second phase of the research paper, an overview of the civil rights movement during the 1960s. The paper asserted that during these years blacks had common goals but advocated different methods of achieving them. I had not seen this draft in progress and, upon reading it, was pleasantly surprised. It was organized, focused, and well-supported, and Diane had written it on her own.

But there was another change. As well as representing an advance in higher-order skills, this paper showed that in the course of our conferences, Diane, like the students whom Susanna Horn mentions in chapter 10, had increased her mastery of lower-order skills. Comparing this paper with examples of her writing from the early fall term, I found that the current paper's vocabulary and writing style were mature and that the sentence structure was more varied and interesting. This advancement in skill was not an obvious result of our work in the writing center, for we only occasionally had time to polish her style. Then I remembered that Diane herself had begun to direct my attention to problem areas in her papers. "I know this sentence is really bad," she would say. Or, "There isn't a very good transition here. What can I do?" She had become aware of what good writing was and, most important, had decided that her own work had possibilities. Two terms of classroom instruction and the comments of her peer writing group, plus the exposure to professional writing that she had experienced from doing her research, undoubtedly contributed to this awareness. But the practice in expressing ideas verbally, which she rarely did in class, and the opportunity in a pressure-free environment to hear me say, "I don't follow you—explain it again," without her becoming embarrassed before a group, helped Diane spot her own weaknesses and move beyond the novice stage toward that of a competent practitioner.

Diane's second paper came back with the instructor's warning, "You are on the verge of writing a report. Be sure you have a thesis that is arguable." The final phase of the research project was to be a sharply focused paper interpreting one specific area or event. Diane could no longer avoid committing herself to an assertion. She returned to an event that especially fascinated her: the Birmingham riots of 1963. "Why," she asked, "had blacks been so viciously attacked during a peaceful demonstration? What were the causes for the blacks' discontent and the whites' violent reaction?" Her research was done; she now had to interpret and develop her argument. Again, I wanted to avoid being too directive, but my caution proved unnecessary. Diane had become so involved in trying to unravel the causes of the Birmingham riots that she had a concrete thesis statement and a partially completed draft by the time she came to our next session. We talked about higher-order issues, such as the direction of the rest of the paper, the necessity for factual support, and the importance of an effective conclusion, but since the paper was due soon, Diane would have to write the final draft alone.

She stopped by at the end of the quarter to show me the graded final paper, trying to be casual, but obviously proud of the A and the instructor's comment, "This is a *good* essay, Diane. All the thinking paid off." Diane's introduction to the final draft shows that her thinking had indeed produced noticeable results:

> Nineteen sixty three was the beginning of the Civil Rights Movement. The weeks of rioting in Birmingham in May of 1963 made the whites stand up and take notice of the Negroes' demands for equality. . . . The rioting in Birmingham was unparalleled by any other Negro demonstrations. Although the Negroes' demonstration was blamed for the rioting, the revolt was caused by white provocation, the Negro frustration due to the lack of progress in school desegregation, and Negro Civil Rights in general.

During the quarter, I had given Diane little help with actually putting words on paper. We had exchanged ideas, expressed opinions, made connections. I had become tougher with her, pressing her to find support for her ideas and forcing her to clarify her thoughts. I had played devil's advocate many times. But Diane had met my challenges instead of withdrawing; she had learned to believe in herself and in me enough to decide when to defend her writing and when to alter it. She had made a commitment to her position on this issue, giving support to A. L. Brown's observation, "Deep understanding is most likely to occur when students are required to explain, elaborate, or defend their positions to others" (1988, 316). Diane had become more self-directed, and almost spontaneously her writing had improved.

The full impact of Diane's progress struck me one morning during the spring term when Diane, in jeans and letter jacket, bustled in purposefully, opened her notebook, and took out a handful of papers. "I'm writing a paper about this story, 'The Man Who Was Almost a Man.' I have a thesis, but it's not clear enough, and I'm having trouble with the introduction. I'm telling too much of the story. We can work on the thesis first." The same student, six months before, had said, "I guess I just can't write." She still needed help: her ideas sometimes needed to be focused and articulated, and her writing style tended to be a little choppy. However, she was now aware of the process that she followed in writing a paper, and she could develop her ideas independently, confident of having something worthwhile to say.

Working with literature is often very difficult for engineering students, and I had wondered whether Diane would do as well in the spring quarter, but she was full of assurance. Her improved organizational and analytical skills are shown by the complex theses she formulated for her two major papers that term:

> In Richard Wright's story, "The Man Who Was Almost a Man", a young boy, named Dave, more than anything in the whole world wanted to be treated like an adult; he wanted to be a man. Dave associated adulthood with power and thus thought that a gun would give him power to be an adult. What Dave didn't realize was that he would have a hard time being treated like an adult in his community, because of where he was born, how his friends and especially his parents saw him, and because of his distorted view of adulthood.

> In Joseph Heller's novel, *Catch 22,* the total insanity of the war is portrayed by the words and actions of the characters involved. Thrown into a totally insane situation such as a war, people react very differently to the stress that they encounter. Nately was willing to die for his country, while Milo would do anything if there was a profit to be made, and Yossarian was willing to defend his country but only up to a certain point. The basic principles of the men may vary, but they all did what they thought was right in an effort to cope with the insanity of war.

Diane supported both theses logically and coherently, demonstrating her increasing expertise. She now used me as a sounding board, checking already developed concepts against my critical judgment instead of waiting for my direction. This newfound confidence and enthusiasm were reflected in her classroom behavior. Her instructor, whom Diane had been fortunate enough to keep for all three quarters of the composition course, reported that Diane now actively contributed to class discussions and often took the lead in commenting on the papers of other students in her writing group. Diane, in turn, was more enthusiastic about both her class and her teacher. Instead of the occasional references to "what *she* wants," Diane now told me, "My teacher's pretty good. We get along all right."

Not all the credit for Diane's progress can go to our writing conferences, of course. Diane was a serious student, eager to please and open to suggestions despite her reticence; and she had a conscientious, concerned instructor who was always accessible to both Diane and me. Not all students make so much progress, even under the best of circumstances. Nearly all of them, however, agree that the writing conferences and the Writing Lab help them feel more comfortable and confident about their writing. This increased confidence is sometimes translated into better grades, but it is always translated into a feeling of personal accomplishment.

Works Cited

Brown, A. L. 1988. "Motivation to Learn and Understand: On Taking Charge of One's Own Learning." *Cognition and Instruction* 5:311–21.

Freedman, Sarah Warshauer, and Anne Marie Katz. 1987. "Pedagogical Interaction during the Composing Process: The Writing Conference." In *Writing in Real Time: Modeling Production Processes,* ed. Ann Matsuhashi. Norwood, N.J.: Ablex.

Index

Academic discourse, 18–19
Acceptance, atmosphere of, 2–7
Acts of Meaning (Bruner), 19
Actual Minds, Possible Worlds (Bruner), 19
Age, effect on anxiety, 63
Anxiety. *See also* Confidence
  and the counseling approach, 24
  effect on syntax, 62–66, 67
  and questioning, 45
  strategies for overcoming, 65–66, 67–68
Appreciation of literature (response to poetry). *See* Poetry
Authority (control). *See also* Independence; Ownership
  in collaboration, 11
  and construction of knowledge, 20
  and conversation, 17, 21
  and the counseling approach, 25–26, 27
  and questioning, 22, 37, 41, 42, 44–45, 49, 50
  and response to poetry, 78–79
  sharing of, 11, 17, 20–21, 50

Bader, M. S., 99–100
Bartholomae, David, 66
Belenky, Mary Field, 84
Benjamin, Alfred, 37
Bereiter, Carl, 55–56
Bizzell, Patricia, 83
Bleich, David, 18, 20, 77
Bos, Candace S., 100
Brannon, Lil, 25
Brooklyn Plan, 19, 70
Brown, A. L., 117
Bruffee, Kenneth A., 3, 6, 18, 19, 21, 70
Bruner, Jerome, 18, 19–20, 35
Buss, Arnold H., 62–63

Caring and warmth, 27
Carter, Michael, 18

Challenge response, 57, 84–87
Client-Centered Therapy (Rogers), 25
Clinchy, Blythe, 83
Cognition
  apprenticeship for growth in, 53–54
  in response to questioning, 38, 39
Cognitive science, findings on tutorials in, 3, 6
Collaborative relationship
  and authority, 11
  counseling approach to, 21, 26, 27
  and independence, 11
  and learning, 19
  and questioning, 22
Conference on College Composition and Communication, 103
Confidence, 8, 111–12, 114, 118, 119. *See also* Anxiety
Content. *See* Meaning (content)
Control. *See* Authority (control)
Conversation. *See also* Dialogue; Listening and understanding, techniques for; Questioning
  and authority, 17, 21
  in construction of knowledge, 17, 18
  social conversation vs. writing conference, 11
Correctness and meaning, 92–93, 94, 103, 107–9
Cosgrove, Cornelius, 92, 94, 95–102
Counseling concepts, 21–22, 24–32
  and anxiety, 24
  and authority, 25–26, 27
  and construction of knowledge, 24
  helping relationship in, 27, 30
  listening and understanding techniques, 24, 29, 30–32
  summary of, 28–29
Critique, social interaction for, 9
Culture and language, 20. *See also* Dialect shift

Dialect shift, 92, 103-9
Dialogue, features and function of, 9, 10.
    See also Conversation; Listening and
    understanding, techniques for;
    Questioning
Dillon, J. T., 37, 39
Direct instruction, 91, 92
Discourse, academic, 18-19
Dissonance, 35, 36, 38-39
Double Perspective (Bleich), 20
Dreyfus, Hubert L., 54, 61
Dreyfus, Stuart E., 54, 61
Dualistic intellectual framework, 83, 85

Editing. *See* Self-editing
Emig, Janet, 21, 92
Empathy, 27
Error
    and dialect, 92, 103-9
    emphasis on, effect on meaning, 92-93,
        94, 103, 107-9
    in grammar, 99, 103, 105-8
    higher-order thinking for reduction of, 8,
        92, 116
    in syntax, 62-66, 67, 99
Expertise. *See also* Novice-expert
    interaction
    definition of, 18-19
    in productive dialogue, 10
    steps in progress toward, 54-55

Faigley, Lester, 67
Felt need, 35, 36, 38-39
Flanders, N., 11
Fletcher, David C., 17, 22, 24, 34, 39-40,
    41-50
Flexibility, 8
Flower, Linda, 9
Flynn, Thomas, 3-14, 80
*Forms of Intellectual and Ethical
    Development in the College Years: A
    Scheme* (Perry), 82-83
Freedman, Sarah Warshauer, 4, 11, 115
Freewriting
    in anxiety/syntax research, 64
    dialect-related errors in, 104
    with learning-disabled students, 100
    in response to poetry, 75
Freire, Paolo, 6, 45, 70

Garrison, Roger H., 4
Geertz, Clifford, 6, 19
Gender in anxiety/syntax correlations, 65,
    67
Grammar
    and dialect, 103, 104-8
    and self-editing, 99, 103, 105-8
Graves, Donald H., 4

Harris, Muriel, 3
Hatano, Giyoo, 53
Hays, Janice N., 84
Heath, Shirley Brice, 18, 20
Helping Interview, The (Benjamin), 37
Helping relationship, conditions for, 27,
    30. *See also* Counseling concepts
Heuristics
    in general, 56, 57
    for response to literature, 71, 75-77, 78
Higher-order thinking. *See also* Intellec-
    tual development
    and confidence, 112
    definition of, 67, 93-94
    elements of instruction for, 3, 7
    in improvement of lower-order skills, 8,
        92, 116
    and independence, 93
    and questioning, 39, 48-49
Hillocks, George, Jr., 4-5
Horn, Susanna, 8, 66, 92-93, 94, 103-10
Hurlow, Marcia L., 55, 56, 62-68, 77

Imperatives in conference strategy, 39
Inagaki, Kayoko, 53
Independence, 7, 8, 10-11, 91-94
Indirect leading (listening technique), 32
Individualized instruction, 4-5
Insecurity. *See* Anxiety; Confidence
Intellectual development
    Perry's model of, 82-84
    writing conference for, 84-87
Irish, Gayle, 108-9

Johnson, JoAnn B., 10, 17, 22, 34-40, 42,
    85

Katz, Anne Marie, 11, 115
King, Mary, 55, 56-57, 69-79

Knowledge, social construction of
and counseling approach, 24
sharing authority for, 20
theory of, 6, 19, 70
through conversation, 17, 18
Knowledge-telling strategy, 55–57, 77
Knowledge-transforming strategy, 55–57
Kuhn, Thomas, 19

Language and culture, 20
Leading, indirect (listening technique), 32
Learning disabilities
definition of, 95–97
serving students with, 92, 97–101
Lerner, Janet W., 99
Linguistic competence and dialect, 103
Listening and understanding, techniques
for, 24, 29, 30–32
Literature, appreciation of (response to
poetry). *See* Poetry
Lives on the Boundary (Rose), 24
Lower-order thinking
higher-order thinking for improvement
of, 8, 92, 116
and questioning, 42, 49

McKoski, Martin, 19
Meaning (content)
construction of, 18, 19, 93
and correctness, 92–93, 94, 103, 107–9
and higher-order thinking, 6
and questioning, 47–48
Modeling, social interaction for, 9
Motivation, social interaction for, 9
Moulton, J. R., 99–100
Moursund, Janet P., 37–38
Multiple-source papers, 57, 80–87
Multiplistic intellectual framework, 83, 85
Murray, Donald M., 4, 30
Mutuality, 20

Need, felt, 35, 36, 38–39
"Non-Magical Thinking: Presenting
Writing Developmentally in Schools"
(Emig), 21
Novice, characteristics of, 54. *See also*
Novice-expert interaction
Novice-expert interaction. *See also*
Conversation; Questioning
dialogue in, 9, 10

and higher-order thinking, 7, 8
intellectual development through, 84–87
overview of strategies for, 53–57
in response to poetry, 73, 78
theoretical basis for, 18

Outlines, 60
Ownership. *See also* Authority
and questioning, 50
and response to poetry, 74, 77–78
Oye, Paula M., 7–8, 9–10, 24, 49, 66, 93,
94, 111–19

Palinscar, Annemarie Sullivan, 10, 11
Paraphrasing (listening technique), 29, 31,
39
Peer tutoring, 19, 99
Perception checking (listening technique),
29, 31–32
Perry, William G., 82–84
Piaget, Jean, 21, 35
Poetry, 57, 69–79
aesthetic response to, 74, 78
definition of, 73
nonaesthetic reading of, 73–74
and reader-response theory, 57, 70–71,
73, 78–79
Power. *See* Authority (control)
Process-oriented instruction, 100–101

Questioning
discussion of problems with, 22, 34, 36–
40
and dissonance, 35, 36, 38–39
emotional messages in, 37
in establishing authority, 22, 41, 42, 44–
45, 49, 50
and higher-order thinking, 39, 48–49
results of research on, 22, 36–38

Reader, the Text, and the Poem, The
(Rosenblatt), 71, 73–74, 75, 78
Reader-response theory, 70–71, 73, 78–79
Regard and respect, 27, 30
Reik, Theodor, 30
Relativistic intellectual framework, 83–
84, 86
Research papers, 114–17
Resnick, Lauren, 6–7, 9, 93–94

Respect and regard, 27, 30
Rogers, Carl, 21, 25, 27, 30, 35
Rorty, Richard, 6, 19
Rose, Mike, 24, 69, 72, 78, 98
Rosenblatt, Louise M., 71, 73–74, 75, 77, 78
Rowe, Mary Budd, 38

Scaffolding, 9, 11
Scardamalia, Marlene, 55–56
Schmitzer, Thomas C., 54, 55, 59–61, 68
Self-Consciousness and Social Anxiety (Buss), 62–63
Self-editing
    and dialect shift, 103, 105–8
    oral reading for, 99, 107–8
Sentence combining, 66
Slattery, Patrick J., 50, 53, 55, 56–57, 80–87
Smitherman-Donaldson, Geneva, 103, 109
Social construction of knowledge. *See* Knowledge, social construction of
Social conversation vs. writing conference, 11
Social interaction in instruction
    benefits of, 9
    and higher-order thinking, 7–8
    theory of, 9–10
Sociocognitive concepts, 9–10
Style development, 113–14
Summarizing (listening technique), 32
Support response, 57, 84–86
Syntax
    effect of anxiety on, 62–66, 67
    self-editing for, 99

Task Force on Curriculum Design and Construction, 109
Taylor, David, 10, 17, 21–22, 24–33, 34, 68, 111, 112
Teachable moment, 59
Telling knowledge, 55–57, 77
Therapist, writing instructor as, 25–26

Thesis development, 115–16
Tompkins, Jane, 70
Transforming knowledge, 55–57
Transmission model of teaching, 45
Trillin, Calvin, 26
Trimbur, J., 3, 6
Trust, atmosphere of, 24, 27
Tutorials, overview of research on, 3. *See also* Writing conference

Understanding. *See* Listening and understanding, techniques for
University of Akron Writing Center, 36–38, 71–72

Validation, social interaction for, 9
Vygotsky, L. S., 35

Warmth and caring, 27
Ways with Words (Heath), 20
Weiner, Eva S., 99
Women's Ways of Knowing: The Development of Self, Voice, and Mind (Belenky), 84
Writing conference. *See also* Novice-expert interaction
    for developing confidence, 8, 111–12, 114, 118, 119
    features of, 4
    independence through, 7, 8, 10–11, 91–94
    intellectual development through, 84–87
    with learning-disabled students, 99–100
    models for, 34–35
    overview of research on, 4–6
    sociocognitive foundations of, 9–10
    stages of, 28–29

Youngstown State University Writing Center, 59–61

Zimmerman, Claire, 83

Editors

Thomas Flynn is Associate Professor of English at Ohio University—Eastern. His professional activities include presiding over the East Central Writing Centers Association, helping to write the K-12 Ohio Language Arts Curriculum, and, for the last thirteen years, chairing the James Wright Poetry Festival. In addition to those responsibilities, he is involved in other diverse aspects of literacy, such as writing poetry with second graders and studying the sociocognitive processes of expert writers.

Mary King directs the Writing Lab and the Basic Writing program at the University of Akron. She has helped organize and staff a community tutorial program for public school students; has chaired the executive board of the East Central Writing Centers Association; has served on the boards of Akron's and Ohio's NCTE affiliates; and has presented papers at meetings of the Writing Centers Association, the National Conference on Basic Writing, and the Conference on College Composition and Communication. Her greatest interest is in observing how people create knowledge during conversation and in researching the relationship between that cognitive process and the learning promoted by acts of writing; as a result, she finds working with students in the Writing Lab to be the most rewarding of her professional activities.

Contributors

Cornelius Cosgrove is Associate Professor of English at Slippery Rock University of Pennsylvania. He directs that university's Writing Center and serves on the executive board of the East Central Writing Centers Association. Previously he taught writing in a two-year college and a high school. He has published articles in such journals as *Teaching English in the Two-Year College* and *English Leadership Quarterly*. In addition, he has presented papers at the annual convention of the Conference on College Composition and Communication, the Penn State Conference on Composition and Rhetoric, and various regional and state conferences.

David C. Fletcher has directed the Lehman College Writing Center, CUNY, cotaught the peer tutor preparation course, and provided advisory assistance to area high school and college writing centers for the past seven years. In 1986 he founded the City University of New York Writing Centers Association, which he cochaired for three years. He is also a computer consultant for high school and college writing programs and recently coauthored *Let's Write,* a teacher's guide for developing cross-discipline computer-assisted instruction. He has made numerous presentations at meetings of NECC, NCTE, and CCCC and at regional and local writing center conferences.

Susanna Horn trains and supervises the peer tutors for the Basic Writing program at the University of Akron. She is a faculty tutor in the Writing Lab at Akron, where she also teaches basic writing. She recently collaborated on a sentence-combining book. She has also taught English in public schools and has made a number of presentations at conferences of the East Central Writing Centers Association.

Marcia L. Hurlow is Professor of English and Journalism at Asbury College in Wilmore, Kentucky. Her B.A. in English is from Baldwin-Wallace College, Berea, Ohio. After serving as assistant editor of *The Charolais Way,* she received an M.A. in journalism and a Ph.D. in rhetoric and applied linguistics from Ohio State University. She taught at Southern Oregon State College and Ohio's Urbana College; then she joined the faculty at Asbury College and completed an M.F.A. in creative writing at Vermont College. She has published numerous articles on the teaching of composition, journalism, and creative writing. Her first collection of poetry,

Aliens Are Intercepting My Brain Waves, was published in 1991 and won the State Street Press contest.

JoAnn B. Johnson is Instructor of English Composition at the University of Akron and Kent State University. She has worked in the writing centers at both universities as well as in the Akron City Public Schools. In addition, she has served as a judge in the Power of the Pen Writing Contest for the Akron schools.

Paula M. Oye has been a tutor in the Reading/Writing Center and a teacher of first-year English at Michigan Technological University. In addition, she has privately tutored adult English as a Second Language students and has taught in the Portage Lake Community Schools' adult education program. She is coauthor of a series of reading comprehension workbooks for grades 1–6. She has since left academia.

Thomas C. Schmitzer is Instructor at both Youngstown State University and at Kent State University. He currently holds a lectureship at Kent State, where he teaches advanced composition, Shakespeare, and world literature.

Patrick J. Slattery is Assistant Professor of English at the University of Arkansas, where he teaches graduate and undergraduate courses in composition. Previously he was Associate Director of Composition at the University of Michigan. He has contributed articles to *College Composition and Communication, Journal of Basic Writing, Journal of Teaching Writing,* and *Rhetoric Review* and is coauthor of *Reading, Thinking, and Writing with Sources.*

David Taylor is Associate Professor of English and Director of the Writing Center at Moravian College in Bethlehem, Pennsylvania. He has conducted holistic scoring workshops for high school English teachers. In addition to writing journal articles and book chapters, he collaborated with Anthony D. Fredericks on *Parent Programs in Reading: Guidelines to Success.* His recent sabbatical was spent as a feature writer for *Scuba Diving* and *Outside* magazines.